Six new AMERICAN HERITAGE JUNIOR LIBRARY books are published each year. Titles currently available are:

Men of Science and Invention

Naval Battles and Heroes

Thomas Jefferson and his World

Discoverers of the New World

Railroads in the Days of Steam

Indians of the Plains

The Story of Yankee Whaling

MEN OF SCIENCE
AND INVENTION

ILLUSTRATED WITH PAINTINGS, PRINTS, DRAWINGS,
AND PHOTOGRAPHS OF THE PERIOD

AMERICAN HERITAGE
JUNIOR LIBRARY

MEN OF SCIENCE
AND INVENTION

by the editors of AMERICAN HERITAGE
The Magazine of History

narrative by MICHAEL BLOW
in consultation with ROBERT P. MULTHAUF
Head Curator
Department of Science and Technology
Smithsonian Institution
Washington, D. C.

Published by

AMERICAN HERITAGE PUBLISHING CO., INC., NEW YORK

Book Trade Distribution by

GOLDEN PRESS · NEW YORK

FOREWORD

THIS BOOK will probably be read by the light of an electric lamp, perhaps by a reader who does not remember ever using any other kind of artificial illumination. Americans would not live as we do today without the electric lamp, the telephone, the automobile, and a multitude of other things which were new-fangled in the times of our grandparents. Most of us think of the majority of them as American inventions, and feel satisfied that we are so much cleverer than other people, without wondering why. Some of us do wonder, though; and others should wonder, for it is the person who knows where he has been who is most likely to know where he is going.

The reader will learn that our heroes—Edison, Bell, Henry Ford—did not always just pick up their tools and make an invention. Edison was one of the few who occasionally did just that. But many of them instead thought of a way to make an invention available to everyone, rather than just to the chosen few who could afford an expensive toy. It was in devising ways to make inventions useful to everyone—in mass production—that Americans have excelled.

So it is better for Americans to know something about science and invention than simply to have faith in our inventiveness. For behind most inventions, and behind nearly all of them in the 20th century, lies science. In this background Americans were less prominent in the days of Edison, Bell, and Ford. Science did not seem to make something which was useful to everyone; at least, our grandfathers did not think so. But the Europeans, who often regarded inventions as toys, thought science was more interesting. They spent the 19th century filling books with observations of nature and the way it works. These books spread throughout the world, and answered the questions which puzzled our inventors. And so the story of the electric lamp does not begin with Edison, nor that of the telephone with Bell.

But some Americans also thought science was more interesting. Joseph Henry was one, and Willard Gibbs another. They paid some of the debt American invention owed to European science. In the present century more and more Americans have recognized that science is both interesting and important. And as the exploration of our geographical frontiers has drawn to a close we have found no less excitement in the exploration of the endless frontier of science.

ROBERT MULTHAUF

FIRST EDITION

LIBRARY OF CONGRESS CATALOG CARD NUMBER: 60–13853

The Pope Orrery (above) contains a model of the solar system in which the planets move by clockwork. Built in 1787 by Joseph Pope, its case is decorated with statues of Franklin and Newton, probably cast by Paul Revere.

CONTENTS

THE COLONIES AWAKE

"I could make anything a body wanted," boasted the ingenious lad in Mark Twain's *A Connecticut Yankee in King Arthur's Court*, "anything in the world. If there wasn't any quick new-fangled way to make a thing, I could invent one."

As clever as he was cocky, the Connecticut Yankee became a symbol of inventiveness in the second half of the nineteenth century. And why not? Americans, it seemed, had invented nearly everything there was to invent. Around the middle of the century, the story goes, a Patent Office official resigned because there was nothing left to invent.

The Connecticut Yankee's confidence may have been well-founded in those days, but it would have astonished the first American settlers. When the first permanent colonies were established in America, there was little time for science and invention. The settlers had their

In 1752 when this painting was made, colonial Baltimore was typical of many American towns on the Atlantic coast. It had little overland trade and no manufacture and had to support itself chiefly with farming and fishing.

hands full building homes, planting enough corn to last through the winter, and keeping marauding Indians at arm's length.

Yet these very time-consuming conditions were a challenge to the settlers who put a high premium on labor-saving tools from the very beginning. The Pilgrims, who came from England via Holland—then one of the leading nations of the world in science and technology— unloaded 102 precious tools from the *Mayflower*. They were hard workers and the colony soon thrived.

The Jamestown colony, founded in 1607, was less fortunate. Its "gentlemen" settlers, sent over to search for gold, collected herbs for drugs, and foraged for other valuable products. They were no match for the wilderness, and the colony nearly perished. In 1609, plagued by famine and Indians, Captain John Smith wrote desperately to England: "I entreat you to send me thirty carpenters, hus-

King Charles II, whose bust appears in the center of this engraving, was the founder of the Royal Society, England's oldest scientific organization.

bandmen, blacksmiths, masons, and diggers up of trees' roots rather than a thousand such as we have."

Soon skilled workers, including Dutchmen sent over to erect sawmills, began to outnumber gentle-men on the ships coming over from England, and the future of Jamestown, the oldest permanent English colony in America, was assured.

Confronted with the hazards of life in a wilderness, the colonists began to improvise on their European implements. They had brought the axe along from England, for example, but it was a heavy clumsy tool that gave the settlers trouble in the dense forests of America. So they made the blade sharper and enlarged the poll, or heavy hammer part, to give the axe better balance and bite. With the new broadaxe, as it was called, Americans made clearings in the wilderness so that crops could be planted.

But because they had to work almost continuously to survive, and were poor in roads and schools, the settlers fell behind Europe in science itself. The art of planting corn was of far more importance to them than speculating on the nature of the universe. Ironically, a great age of "Enlightenment," of knowledge and science, was getting under way in Europe just as many of the first colonists were leaving for America. It began in the middle of the sixteenth century when a Polish scientist, Nicolaus Copernicus, published a book called *On the Revolutions of Heavenly Spheres*. In it he proposed what then seemed unbelievable: the earth and the other planets revolve around the sun.

Ever since ancient times almost everybody had believed that the earth, inhabited by God's most noble creation man, occupied a unique position in the heavens. It was supposed to stand absolutely still at the center of the universe while the moon, the planets, the sun, and stars circled around it. The models scientists contrived to illustrate this Ptolemaic system (it had been advanced by Ptolemy of Alexandria in the second century A.D.) were so impossibly intricate that some men refused to believe that the universe could be so complicated. According to legend, Alfonso the Wise of Spain commented dryly in the thirteenth century that "if the Lord Almighty had consulted me before embarking upon the Creation, I should have recommended something simpler."

John Winthrop
the Younger

Cotton Mather

13

The Industrial Revolution began much earlier in England than it did in America because of England's head start in scientific research. Newcomen engines like this one were used in English coal mines in the early 1700's to pump water from shafts and lift loads of coal.

The Copernican system was a simpler explanation of the movements of heavenly bodies. "In the midst of all dwells the sun," Copernicus wrote, "and so, as if seated upon a royal throne, the sun rules the family of planets as they circle around him."

So the earth became just another planet, and man was dethroned from his proud position at the center of the universe. Both the Protestant and Catholic churches opposed these radical ideas, but it was not long before Copernicus' theories began to receive support as scientists peered at the heavens through the newly invented telescope. This invention is usually credited to the Dutch spectaclemakers, but it was the Italian scientist Galileo Galilei who first used it as a scientific instrument.

When Galileo pointed his telescope toward the heavens, a new world flashed into view. The moon, he discovered, was not a perfect polished sphere but rather pitted and "corrupted" with mountains and valleys just like the earth. In the mysterious white veil of the Milky Way he saw nothing more than innumerable stars, too far away to be seen distinctly with the naked eye.

Pointing his glass toward the sun he saw strange dark blotches—sunspots—moving across its surface.

But his most important discovery was the sighting of four moons circling around Jupiter. Here was a model of the solar system itself, convincing proof that it was organized the way Copernicus had theorized. But there were many who refused to accept Galileo's evidence.

In 1632, when Galileo published his *Dialogue on the Two Chief World Systems*, outlining his many proofs of the Copernican system, matters took a serious turn. He was sum-

moned to Rome by the Inquisition and forced to recant: "I bend my knee before the honourable inquisitor general . . . I abjure and curse the stated heresies," he swore in public. "But," Galileo is said to have said to himself, "The earth *does* move."

Other great scientists of the age helped to knock down the barriers to knowledge. Francis Bacon's philosophical writings—he suggested that scientific knowledge be verified not from scripture but from observation and experiment—stimulated the founding of the Royal Society of London in 1662.

Members of the Royal Society heard such famous scientists as Robert Boyle and Robert Hooke discuss their theories and listened to other members debate the works of Johannes Kepler. This friend of Galileo's had shown that the planets orbit in ellipses rather than circles

A famous English poet, Alexander Pope, wrote a couplet about another member of the Royal Society:

Nature and Nature's laws lay
   hid in night;
God said 'let Newton be,' and
   all was light.

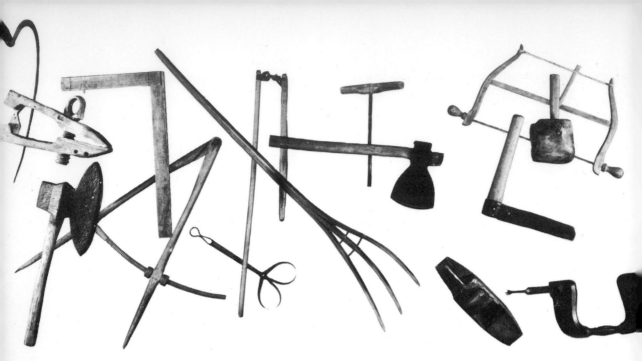

While England was in the midst of building factories, Americans were still making tools like these, by hand, for use on their farms.

Pope was not exaggerating. Isaac Newton's *Mathematical Principles of Natural Philosophy*, published in 1687, was, like the ancient book of Ptolemy, an attempt to describe the heavenly motions mathematically. It is considered the greatest scientific book of all time. In it he formulated his three laws of motion, which describe the movement of all objects, on earth as well as in the heavens. One of them—"every action has an equal and opposite reaction"—was the clue to many future inventions, including jets and rockets.

But Newton's master stroke was his law of universal gravitation. While Newton was unable to say what caused gravity (nobody really can even today), he did explain how it worked, and formulated the force of attraction between any two bodies in the universe.

Suddenly the world of Copernicus, Galileo, and Kepler made sense. Here was mathematical proof of what a handful of men had suspected—that the force which tugs an apple from a tree to the ground is the same force which keeps the moon from flying off into space.

The European scientists of the seventeenth century amassed a vast store of knowledge. Inventors were to draw upon this knowledge for centuries. Word of the new discoveries crossed the ocean to America, but only to a handful of intellectuals in the larger cities, and sometimes rather slowly. The first copy of Newton's *Mathematical Principles* arrived in the colonies in 1708, more than 20 years after publication.

Teaching the new world view was difficult, moreover, for the colonies had no system of public schools, and very few private and church schools. A century after the Jamestown colony was founded only three colleges existed—Harvard, William and Mary, and Yale.

The function of these colleges was largely to graduate ministers for the various churches in the colonies, and courses in science were few and far between. Harvard was the first to set up a position for a professor of mathematics and science, but the first holder of this chair did little to further the cause of science. He was "ejected" for "excessive drinking to the dishonour of God."

Yet even without the knowledge of the mechanical principles that were being formulated by the scientists in Europe, the settlers began to show what came to be known as Yankee inventiveness.

The wooden mouldboard (the curved part of the plow which turns over the sod) was lined with iron, making a stronger, more effective plow. By the middle of the seventeenth century shipbuilders along the seaboard developed a new type of sailing vessel called the ketch, and not long after that the schooner. The famous Conestoga wagon that the settlers used on their westward treks was an improvement on an English design.

Weapons were devised that particularly suited the needs of the colonists. In Pennsylvania, Swiss and German immigrants developed the "Kentucky" rifle. European smoothbore muskets were too inaccurate and short-ranged to be effective against Indians or game at any distance. The Pennsylvania gunsmiths "rifled" the barrel so that the projectile would spin, thus gaining accuracy and lengthened the barrel so that the bullet would carry farther.

The long rifle was so effective at picking off British sentries and officers during the Revolution that a printer in Philadelphia wrote to a friend in London: "I advise your officers who shall . . . come out to America to settle their affairs in England before their departure."

American industry boomed right along with Yankee ingenuity. In 1720 the shipwrights in London complained to the King that they were receiving too much competition from Yankee shipbuilders who were then sending ships down the ways faster than any other nation in the world. Iron forges sprang up all over the colonies, and after 1722 not a single axe was imported from England by New England, New York, or Pennsylvania. Iron, in fact, was being exported to England.

The "Kentucky rifle" was developed by colonial gunsmiths in Pennsylvania.

Water wheels like these provided power for American industry before the advent of the steam engine. This painting shows the famous Du Pont gunpowder mills, near Wilmington, Delaware, in 1800.

The British were first amazed and then alarmed. A colony, they felt, ought to supply the mother country with raw materials, and then provide a market for the goods the mother country manufactures.

British ironmakers followed the example of the London shipwrights and petitioned Parliament not to allow Americans to make axe heads, shovels, nails, and many other products. But the Iron Act of 1750, one of the causes of the Revolution, did not stop American progress. In 1776 America was ahead of England and behind only Sweden and Russia, in the manufacture of iron.

As the colonies prospered, and

Americans began to feel they could make anything they needed themselves, a few men appeared who were interested in science for its own sake, in research, and in discovering the secrets of the universe.

One of the first was John Winthrop the Younger, the son of the great Puritan governor of Massachusetts. Winthrop had emigrated to the colonies in 1631, but he traveled to England periodically, and on one of these trips he had helped to found the Royal Society.

In 1662, on one of his return trips, Winthrop brought back a telescope three-and-a-half feet long. For ten years the amiable governor of Connecticut kept the late hours of an astronomer, peering through his rather ungainly glass at the heavenly bodies. Primitive as his telescope was, Winthrop claimed to have spotted the fifth of Jupiter's twelve

The sturdy Conestoga wagon first appeared in America in the 1750's. It was designed with a watertight bottom for fording streams and could haul heavy loads.

moons, a sighting that was not made again for more than 200 years.

Like many an American scientist to follow him, Winthrop also turned his mind to industry. In 1635 he set up a "chymist's" plant to make alum for curing skins and saltpeter for gunpowder. He also learned how to mine lead, tin, and copper.

But it was his work in astronomy, mathematics, and chemistry that earned him the respect of the Royal Society. The Society's journal, *Philosophical Transactions*, was to report that only the end of the Civil War in England, around 1650, kept the scientists from picking up shop and moving to the "new-born colony" of John Winthrop the Younger.

In 1672 Winthrop gave his telescope to Harvard College where it was used by another pioneer American astronomer, Thomas Brattle. His observations on comets were passed on to Isaac Newton, who used the

information in his *Mathematical Principles*.

One of Brattle's antagonists in later years was a stout Congregational minister, Cotton Mather, whom many remember only as the instigator of the witch trials in Salem, Massachusetts. Cotton Mather firmly believed in witchcraft, and he wrote several treatises on the treatment and punishment of those "diabolically possessed." He also had the rather unscientific notion that when pigeons migrated in the winter they flew up to some "undiscovered satellite accompanying the earth at a near distance."

Yet Mather had a fine scientific mind in many other ways. His learned papers on the biology of plants brought him membership in the Royal Society. When a smallpox epidemic struck Boston in 1721, Mather was one of the few to urge the new system of inoculation.

Prefacing one of his medical studies, Mather wrote modestly that he did not expect that the colonies, while "yett so much in their infancy as ours are, . . . can be so circumstanced as to produce many acute mathematicians, or allow them the leisure for extraordinary inventions and performances."

But perhaps he was too modest, for while most of the colonists did not even know about the discoveries the scientists were making, they nevertheless continued to invent new tools and methods of manufacturing them. Gradually they began to feel that their ideas were worth something, that the invention of their minds entitled them to certain rights.

The first patent in the New World was granted by the Massachusetts General Court in 1641 to a man named Samuel Mills for "a new method of making salt." Five years later the first patent on a piece of machinery was granted by the same court to Joseph Jenks for "engines for mills to go by water for the speedy dispatch of much work with few men's labor in little time," and a "now invented sawmill . . ."

Jenks had been brought over from England by Winthrop to work in his iron foundries, and he is perhaps the first of the breed of American inventor-capitalists who were to appear in such great numbers in the nineteenth century. For although Jenks continued to work in Winthrop's foundry, he purchased the right to set up his own forge and went into business for himself.

The first Massachusetts patents were not really patents at all in the modern sense of the word. They were issued only by special acts of the legislature after the inventor had made an appeal to the governing body of his colony. The legislatures of the colonies were very much afraid of establishing "monopolies" of the kind granted by European kings. They granted patents only for "such new inventions as were profitable to the country," and these for a short time only.

But gradually the feeling that a man was entitled to certain rights on his invention overcame the fear of monopoly. When the delegates of the thirteen states met in 1787 to frame the Constitution, one of the problems before them was how to grant proper patents.

On September 17, 1787, the Constitution was signed and it contained this provision: "Congress shall have power . . . to promote the progress of science and the useful arts by securing for limited times to . . . inventors the exclusive right to their . . . inventions." All the patent acts since stem from this declaration.

With new tools and goods being made it was not long before Americans devised a way to sell them. The gospel of free enterprise in the colonies grew up with a character called the Yankee peddler or, to use the name folklore gave him in the nine-

Peddlers like the top-hatted man in this picture were welcome visitors to
the isolated farms and small villages of early America. The peddler carried
pots, pans, needles, cloth, candlesticks — all of the things that could not be
made at home or bought in country stores — in his horse-drawn cart. He
was the man who carried America's first manufactured goods to the consumers.

teenth century, Sam Slick of Pumpkin Crick.

The fast-talking, nattily-dressed, top-hatted Yankee peddler roamed the country by horse-drawn wagon or on foot, a traveling salesman of colonial days. His best items were clocks from Connecticut, and he also distributed wooden egg beaters, apple parers, meat mincers, and nutmeg grinders.

The Yankee peddler helped accustom Americans to the idea of free enterprise, and, in a very basic sense, to the advantages of labor-saving devices. By the time the colonies banded together to form the United States of America the idea of using machines to make life easier was well established.

England, in fact, had already begun to criticize America's "love of luxury." And a young man in Philadelphia felt obliged to write to his uncle in France: "What answer do you have for the growing luxury of my country which gives so much offense to all English travelers without exception?" From France a seventy-eight-year-old statesman, scientist, and inventor named Benjamin Franklin penned this reply:

"Is not the hope of one day being able to purchase and enjoy luxuries a great spur to labor and industry? May not luxury, therefore, produce more than it consumes, if without such a spur people would be, as they are naturally enough inclined to be, lazy and indolent?"

FRANKLIN, RITTENHOUSE, RUMFORD, AND JEFFERSON

Benjamin Franklin was born in Boston in 1706, one of four boys in a family of ten children. He did not seem very bright at first, but he showed promise of becoming a fine athlete. He learned to swim almost as soon as he could walk.

Paddling around a pond as a youth, Franklin tied a kite string to his wrist and, giving the kite an occasional jerk to keep it up, let himself be pulled across the pond by the wind. Not long afterwards he devised "palettes" for the hands and swimming "sandals" for the feet. With these crude frogman flippers he found that he could increase his swimming speed.

But even the ingenuity of these early efforts in the field of transportation gave no hint of Franklin's genius. For almost eighty years afterward his remarkable mind continued to invent and explore the laws of nature. Best known for this work, and as statesman, diplomat, and author, Franklin was also an economist, journalist, printer, mason, musician, publisher, storekeeper, and more than a half a dozen other things as well. At seventy-eight Franklin invented bifocals, and when he was eighty-one he helped to frame the Constitution of the United States.

Of all his activities and accomplishments perhaps his scientific experiments have proved to be the most fruitful for mankind. Yet Franklin had no formal education in science. There was still little to be had in the colonies, but this was no hurdle to the boy from Boston.

At the time little was known about the mysterious sparks that could be made by rubbing a glass rod with fur and putting a finger close to it, although it seemed that other materials had the same curious property. The Englishman William Gilbert, physician to Queen Elizabeth, had shown that amber and sulphur would also store up a shock. Then Otto von Guericke, a portly German burgomaster, devised the first "electrostatic" machine, which was simply a ball of sulphur on a shaft. By spinning the sphere and holding his hand against it a charge could be stored up.

Then an electric bottle called the Leyden jar was developed and soon became the scientific sensation of Europe. In Paris several hundred monks joined hands, and one of them grasped the iron chain leading from a charged Leyden jar. As the shock passed through them all simultaneously, they jerked towards heaven in unison.

Popular interest in Franklin's earlier electrical experiments is seen in this picture of Americans—circa 1790—rubbing rods to produce a charge of static electricity.

Little of this European work was known to Franklin. On a business trip to Boston in 1746, however, Franklin was intrigued by an exhibition of the wonders of electricity put on by a Dr. Spence. His experiments "were imperfectly performed," Franklin reported—but he later bought Spence's apparatus anyway and wrote to England for more.

With this primitive equipment, and more that he built himself, Franklin made a number of major discoveries about the nature of electricity:

Static electricity, Franklin argued (the kind you store up by rubbing your feet on a rug and discharge by touching a doorknob) "leaks" off the body at sharp points such as the fingers. This is now called the point effect.

There is only one kind of electricity instead of the resinous and vitreous types then thought to exist, but this electricity can have either a negative or a positive charge. These plus and minus charges attract each other, Franklin noted, by observing how an electrical spark will jump

Franklin commissioned the first charting of the Gulf Stream in 1769. He advised captains to sail with the current to speed eastward transatlantic crossings and to avoid it when sailing west.

Franklin designed his own bifocal spectacles in 1785. The top half of each lens was used for viewing objects at a distance; the bottom half for reading.

Franklin used equipment like this in the experiment to prove for the first time that electrical sparks produce heat. The Leyden jar (left) supplied the electrical charge which caused a spark to occur in the cylinder (right). A thermometer at the top of the cylinder recorded the increase in heat caused by the spark.

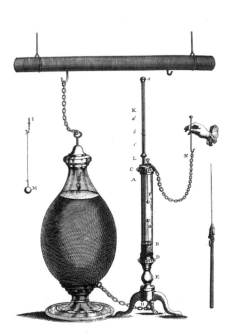

Three wooden models, equipped with lightning rods, demonstrated how Franklin's popular invention made houses and churches safer during electrical storms.

the gap between two oppositely charged terminals.

Lightning is simply a big electric spark. This had been suspected in Europe, but Franklin was the first man to suggest a good proof. He set about experimenting after noting that lightning and the electric spark were alike in many ways. Their shape and color were similar, they seemed to travel at about the same speed, and both destroyed animals. Franklin proposed to build a sort of "sentry box" on a high tower. A man was to stand inside the box on top of an "electrical stand" (an insulated platform) and draw sparks from passing storm clouds with a long pointed iron rod.

Franklin published his proposal, and before he got around to trying it out a French scientist named D'Alibard set up the sentry box experiment outside Paris in 1752. With a peal of thunder and a flash of lightning his iron shaft sparkled blue —"drawing fire from a cloud" as Franklin put it—showing that clouds were electrified.

Franklin tried the same experiment with different apparatus. He fixed a sharp-pointed wire to the top of a kite and hitched a ribbon to the end of the kite string for insulation. Then he knotted a large iron key between the kite string and the length of ribbon.

Franklin invited his twenty-one-year-old son along to take part in the "sport." When a storm cloud passed by, Franklin saw the fibers of the kite string stand on end, and he drew a spark from the key with his knuckle.

The experiment is not recommended for amateurs as a Swedish scientist in Russia who tried a similar experiment not long afterwards found out. A bolt of lightning struck the iron rod he was holding and killed him.

Franklin immediately put the new knowledge to work. The lightning rod, designed to bleed the electric charge off buildings and other structures, began to sprout from colonial rooftops in the 1750's. Its magic left some unconvinced. Boston, the Reverend Thomas Prince pointed out, had more "iron points" than anyplace else in New England, and yet

Many Americans heated their houses with the stove invented by Benjamin Franklin.

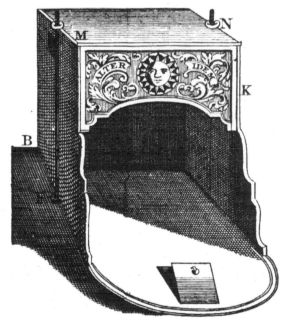

rather ambitious objectives. "The first drudgery of settling the new colonies," he wrote, "is now pretty well over." Let us, he suggested, "improve the common stock of knowledge."

Specifically, Franklin proposed finding new ways of curing diseases and mining ore, improving wines and breeding animals, manufacturing goods and clearing land, and finally, "all philosophical experiments that let light into the nature of things, tend to increase the power of man over matter, and multiply the conveniences or pleasures of life."

Taking his own advice to heart, Franklin plunged into his work on electricity. He had already investigated some of the properties of heat.

It was around 1729 when he was working as a printer in Philadelphia that he determined the absorption of heat by materials of different

was heavily shaken by the earthquake of November, 1755. To Prince this was a sign of God's displeasure. "O," he cried, "there is no getting out of the mighty hand of God! If we think to avoid it in the Air we cannot in the Earth . . ."

In 1743 Franklin had founded the American Philosophical Society with

While traveling through the colonies in 1753 to study the postal system, Franklin kept track of the mileage he covered by attaching an odometer, like that above, to the axle of one of his carriage wheels.

The Comforts of a Rumford Stove.

Vide Dr G___m's Lecture

This cartoon shows the elegant Count Rumford warming himself in front of a Rumford "stove." The stove was actually an improvement on the conventional fireplace and had new features which kept smoke at a minimum and distributed heat evenly.

29

colors. After a snowfall one day, he put squares of cloth of different colors on the snowbanks and let the sun play on them. In a few hours he noticed that a black piece had sunk into the snow the farthest, lighter colored pieces less, and a white piece not at all. Franklin correctly reasoned that dark colors absorb the sun's heat more readily than paler ones, which reflect part of the sun's radiation.

The practical use of this experiment came to mind immediately: people who live in the tropics should wear white clothes. Franklin was also one of the first to verify that evaporating perspiration helps to keep the body cool, and to investigate the rate at which different substances conduct heat. After these experiments he was able to explain why silver teapots, for instance, must be equipped with wooden handles.

But Franklin is perhaps better known for his inventions than for his experiments. His first major one was the Franklin stove. While many people regarded his lightning rod with skepticism, nobody ever doubted that the stove added to the "pleasures of life."

Before Franklin tinkered with the stove, Americans relied upon open fireplaces to heat their homes or upon iron stoves of the German kind. The first sent most of the heat up the chimney and smoke into the room, and the German iron stoves heated the same air over and over until it became barely breathable.

Franklin pulled the stove out from the wall, so that its back and sides would also warm the air in the room, and equipped it with a pipe to carry the fumes up a chimney. The pipe sometimes doubled back on itself forming a kind of crude radiator.

Benjamin Franklin made no attempt to patent his stove or any of his other inventions. "As we enjoy great advantages from the inventions of others," he wrote, "we should be glad to serve others by any inventions of ours."

And serve others he did. Besides the lightning rod and the stove, Franklin invented watertight compartments for ships, a mechanical hand with a long handle for reaching things in high places (we know it today as the grocer's claw), designed ship hulls, and proposed boats powered by jets of water much like those in use today.

His creative mind saw a use and a purpose in invention which often escaped less imaginative men. In Paris in 1783, Franklin watched the balloon made by the Montgolfier brothers lift two men up into the sky for the first time. "Of what possible use can these air balls be?" scoffed a spectator.

"Of what use," replied the seventy-seven-year-old Franklin, "is a newborn baby?"

When Franklin died in 1790, a shy retiring astronomer named

The United States.

To all to whom these Presents shall come. Greeting.

Whereas Samuel Hopkins of the City of Philadelphia and State of Pensylvania hath discovered an Improvement, not known or used before such Discovery, in the making of Pot ash and Pearl ash by a new Apparatus and Process; that is to say, in the making of Pearl ash 1st. by burning the raw Ashes in a Furnace, 2d. by dissolving and boiling them when so burnt in Water, 3rd. by drawing off and settling the Ley, and 4th. by boiling the Ley into Salts which then are the true Pearl ash; and also in the making of Pot ash by fluxing the Pearl ash so made as aforesaid; which Operation of burning the raw Ashes in a Furnace, preparatory to their Dissolution and boiling in Water, is new, leaves little Residuum, and produces a much greater Quantity of Salt: These are therefore in pursuance of the Act, entituled "An Act to promote the Progress of useful Arts", to grant to the said Samuel Hopkins, his Heirs, Administrators and Assigns, for the Term of fourteen Years, the sole and exclusive Right and Liberty of using, and vending to others the said Discovery, of burning the raw Ashes previous to their being dissolved and boiled in Water, according to the true Intent and Meaning of the Act aforesaid. In Testimony whereof I have caused these Letters to be made patent, and the Seal of the United States to be hereunto affixed. Given under my Hand at the City of New York this thirty first Day of July in the Year of our Lord one thousand seven hundred & Ninety.

G Washington

City of New York July 31st. 1790. —

I do hereby Certify that the foregoing Letters patent were delivered to me in pursuance of the Act, entituled "An Act to promote the Progress of useful Arts"; that I have examined the same, and find them conformable to the said Act.

Edm: Randolph Attorney General for the United States. —

(Endorsement on back of grant)

Delivered to the within named Samuel Hopkins this fourth day

August 1790. —

Th Jefferson

The first patent (above) ever issued by the United States was given to Samual Hopkins of Philadelphia for his improvements on the making of "pot ash and pearl ash."

The sketch (below) was made by Rumford as part of a "recipe" for a rocket. He first experimented with gunpowder-charged rockets in America in 1772.

David Rittenhouse took his place as president of the American Philosophical Society. Rittenhouse grew up on his father's farm outside Philadelphia, educated himself, and earned a living as a youth by making clocks. His work was often ignored by Europeans who found it difficult.

In America the skills men learned as clockmakers were often put to use in making engineering devices that would have astounded European artisans. In 1767 Rittenhouse designed and built an orrery—a device which shows the motions of celestial bodies around the sun—which was able to project eclipses and other celestial phenomena for the next 5,000 years, and which could also re-create eclipses which had occurred 5,000 years before its construction.

For the Venus transit, or passage of the planet across the face of the sun in 1769, Rittenhouse put up an

Through the age of Franklin and Jefferson the only important source of industrial power—other than the water wheel—was wind. This is an American windmill of the 1830's.

observatory and built the first telescope made in America. The calculations he made during the transit agree with modern observations, and he was the first to see the Venutian atmosphere.

Rittenhouse's refinements of the telescope and his work on optics brought famous men to his door seeking information or inventions. Jefferson wanted a special kind of pendulum, Franklin an explanation of the scale on his telescope. Nearsighted George Washington asked for and received a decent pair of spectacles.

During the Revolution, Rittenhouse replaced the lead weights on clocks throughout Philadelphia with iron ones so that the Continental Army could use their lead for bullets. Later he served on committees to inspect the Fitch steamboat and a number of other early American engines.

But Rittenhouse was far more than just a tinkerer. His work on optics, magnetism, electricity, and mathematics commanded the attention of the Royal Society. A year before his death in 1796 he was finally elected a member.

If Rittenhouse was the best scientist in America after the death of Franklin, one of the finest in Europe was certainly Count (of the Holy Roman Empire) Rumford, who was born Benjamin Thompson in the little colonial town of Woburn, Massachusetts.

As a child Thompson studied algebra, geometry, and astronomy. His father decided that he was not cut out for life on a farm, and no one could have agreed more than Thompson himself. Apprenticed to a Boston storekeeper, he taught himself how to speak French, dress like a gentleman, and fence like a courtier.

His fantastic career began in 1772 when he married a rich widow in Portsmouth, New Hampshire. Refused a commission in Washington's army (he was suspected of spying for the British—rightly so, it later turned out) Rumford left, in 1776, for England where he engaged in the science of ballistics and designed mortars and rockets.

His work was so brilliant that he was elected a member of the Royal Society at the age of twenty-six. Five years later, in 1784, he was suspected of spying for the French. The British were too embarrassed to come right out and accuse him of it, but things got uncomfortably hot for Thompson in London, and he beat a hasty retreat to the colonies towards the end of the Revolution. When the war was over, he journeyed to Bavaria, where he was made a Count of the Holy Roman Empire.

His was a story of intrigue, adventure, and espionage; yet history will remember Rumford more for his scientific contributions than for his lack of patriotism. For Rumford did for the science of heat what Franklin had done for electricity.

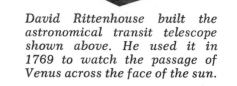

David Rittenhouse built the astronomical transit telescope shown above. He used it in 1769 to watch the passage of Venus across the face of the sun.

The Rittenhouse orrery (above), built in 1767, could indicate the hour, the day, and the year of celestial events such as eclipses, on the faces of its dials.

Having expert knowledge of clocks like the one above, Rittenhouse designed precision instruments used in astronomical observation.

At the time he made his experiments the accepted explanation of heat was that the molecules of every substance were surrounded by an invisible atmosphere of "caloric." When two substances were rubbed together (producing what is now "known as the heat of friction) "caloric" was thought to be squeezed off the surface molecules, thus producing heat.

Thompson demolished this theory with any number of demonstrations. The most famous was the so-called cannon-boring experiment. Measuring the enormous heat that was created by friction in boring out a brass cannon barrel, he showed that it was far too great for the caloric theory to explain. Rumford proved that heat is not a basic property of matter, or a "material substance," but a kind of radiant energy.

Obsessed by the mysterious properties of light and heat, Rumford donated a prize of £1,000 to the Royal Society to be given for the best research in the field over a two-year period. The winner (nobody else was even close) was Count Rumford.

Like Franklin, Rumford put his knowledge to practical use. He invented the modern "non-smoking" fireplace, the drip coffeepot, a pressure cooker, and the thermos bottle (with silvered glass sides to deflect the heat, he reasoned correctly, heat could not flow in or out). Many pots and pans on today's stoves are merely modern versions of "Rumford Roasters." He devised steam radiators and even a form of central heating.

Thompson also gave money to the American Academy of Arts and Sciences where he was elected a member in 1789, and to Harvard College where he studied briefly before leaving the colonies for England. Since his death in 1814, in a little town outside Paris, the two institutions have shared the cost of maintaining the grave of the fortune-seeking rascal who took everything he could from life—and still managed to leave the world a priceless scientific inheritance.

One of Rumford's admirers (his espionage activities remained a secret for more than 150 years) was a young Virginian, Thomas Jefferson, who was the author of the Declaration of Independence, Minister to France, Secretary of State, and third President of the United States. Jefferson, an inspired tinkerer, became the third president of the American Philosophical Society.

The architect of independence was not a scientist in the sense that Franklin and Thompson were, but his inventions show a characteristic American ingenuity. At his beautiful home, Monticello, one can still see some of the gadgets he invented and installed there: a dumb-waiter, a revolving clothes rack, a combination shooting and walking stick, a swivel chair ("so as to look all ways at once," his enemies said). His im-

Benjamin Franklin

Benjamin Thompson, Count Rumford

David Rittenhouse

Thomas Jefferson

provements on the shape of the mouldboard of the plow were based on mathematical principles and were to have an enormous effect on the agricultural development of the country.

More important than these devices, however, was the support and encouragement Jefferson gave to other scientists and inventors. When he was Secretary of State, Jefferson became the first administrator of the nation's new patent system. He never took out a patent himself, believing, as Franklin did, that the fruits of his intellect belonged to everybody.

But he did believe, in spite of the fact that he was against most forms of monopoly, that an inventor should receive protection if he wanted it.

Jefferson also tried to give the new nation a decimal system of coinage and of weights and measures—a system, in other words, in which the different units are related by a ratio of ten. He succeeded with coinage so that today we have ten cents to the dime, and 100 cents to the dollar, rather than the clumsy English system of four farthings to the penny, twelve pence to the shilling, and twenty shillings to the pound. The English are still in the process of trying to change to the decimal system.

Unfortunately, Jefferson failed to unseat the clumsy English system of weights and measures. Today most of the world has adopted the workable metric system developed by French scientists in the 1790's, while the English-speaking lands still fumble with inches and feet, ounces and pounds, and other ancient units with awkward ratios. The system has annoyed scientists seeking uniform precision for centuries, none more than the frustrated German rocket engineers who came to this country after World War II and had to accustom themselves to the archaic English system of measurement.

As Minister to France, Jefferson constantly sent back news of science and invention in Europe. He wrote, in 1785, of a manufacturing system that would have changed the world long before Eli Whitney came up with the idea of interchangeable parts—if anybody paid attention to what he said. "An improvement," he wrote, "is made here in the construction of muskets, which it may be interesting to Congress to know. . . . It consists in the making of every part of them so exactly alike that what belongs to any one may be used for every other musket in the magazine."

Fortunately for Whitney, Jefferson failed to persuade the inventor, a man named Blanc, to come to the United States, and the French failed to adopt the system.

But the subject of another Jefferson report was to change the course of the United States and the whole world. From Europe Jefferson wrote that an Englishman, James Watt, had developed a successful steam engine.

THE INDUSTRIAL REVOLUTION

By the middle of the nineteenth century one could wander through New England and Pennsylvania and see little sign of the inventiveness of the colonists. A cold stone forge lying in the middle of the woods, a deserted windmill, perhaps the bare bones of an old water wheel half sunk in a creekbed—these skeletons of another age were about all that was left. The factories of the Industrial Revolution had taken their place.

The revolution raged for half a century in England before it finally spread to the United States, where it was to reach its greatest development. And although no one thing can be said to have caused it, the greatest force behind it was the power of steam.

They call James Watt the "Father of the Steam Engine," though he was not the first man to make a "fire engine" as they called them in those days. As with most inventions, many men contributed to perfecting and improving it.

A toy steam turbine was described and probably built by Heron of Alexandria about 50 A.D. This device used the power of steam shooting out of little reaction jets to make a ball on top of the boiler rotate. But more than 1,600 years passed before Englishmen were able to put steam to practical use.

Two properties of steam had intrigued men for centuries. One of

America's Industrial Revolution sped up when Eli Whitney began making muskets with interchangeable parts in 1798 at this factory near New Haven, Connecticut.

them was that if you stopped up the spout of a boiling kettle, steam would either pop the stopper out or blow the lid off. On the other hand, if you put boiling water into a bottle, corked it, and let it cool, the stopper would be sucked into the bottle. Nowadays we know the simple explanation for this mysterious behavior. The pressure of expanding steam is responsible for blowing the stopper out of the kettle; when this steam is cooled it condenses, creating a vacuum, and the stopper is shoved into the bottle by the weight of air on top of it.

John Fitch

Oliver Evans

James Watt

After 1650 these curious properties of steam were explored by a number of Englishmen who were trying to develop new types of pumps to remove water from flooded coal mines. One of these engines consisted of an egg-shaped vessel which was alternately filled with steam and water. In these the steam forced the water to a higher level. Others consisted of a cylinder and piston. When a jet of cold water was shot into the cylinder, the steam there condensed, and the piston was forced down by atmospheric pressure.

In 1711 the English blacksmith Thomas Newcomen succeeded in making a successful engine in which the piston was connected to an ordinary suction pump through a "rocking beam" arrangement resembling a teeter-totter. This type of engine was widely used for seventy years to pump out mines (see page 14). One came to the American colonies in 1755.

But about ten years later it began to be replaced by the improved engine of James Watt. Watt saw that too much heat was wasted when cold water was squirted into the cylinder. In order that the cylinder should always "be kept as hot as the steam that enters it," he added a separate condenser. Now the cyl-

"Orukter Amphibolos" (left), an amphibious dredge designed by Oliver Evans, was America's first steam-powered vehicle.

inder did not have to be cooled and reheated with each stroke of the piston. The Watt engine did three times as much work for a given amount of fuel as Newcomen's did.

Watt engines proved useful for other purposes than pumping, and by the end of the century, steam had begun to power English factory workshops. At the same time a number of other Englishmen were engaged in the invention of textile machinery. The spinning machine was developed, and then the power-driven loom. At first the power came from horses or water wheels, but by 1800 the steam engine was also being used to power textile mills. These developments in power and textile machinery, combined with improvements in the making of iron and steel, made up what we call the Industrial Revolution.

In England, where there were too many people and too few jobs, the workers resented the new machines, which caused unemployment and poverty. Each machine might put several men out of work, and they were so simple that even a child could operate them. Unscrupulous English industrialists soon realized this, and eventually four- and five-year-old children worked from dawn to dusk at near-starvation wages.

The workers took their anger out on the machines, breaking and smashing them whenever they had

Fitch's design (below) for using a steam engine to power a ship was granted a patent on November 29, 1791, by King Louis XVI of France.

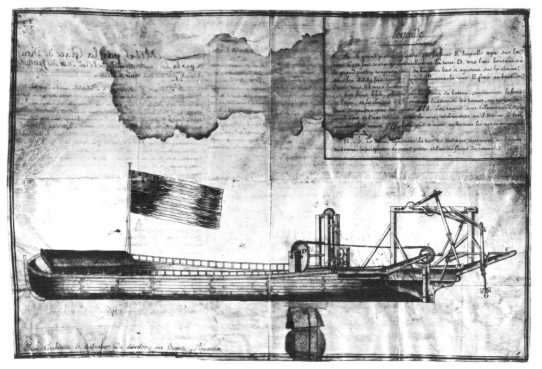

the chance. The situation became so serious that in 1812 the British Parliament was forced to pass a law invoking the death penalty for machine-breaking.

The revolution was a long time in coming to the United States. Britain still would not let her machines—or even the plans for them—out of the country, and skilled craftsmen who worked in the textile mills were not allowed to leave England, either.

But America was ready for the Industrial Revolution. With a relatively small population, and with most of a continent still waiting to be explored and industrialized, Americans came to look upon machines as useful tools, not instruments of the devil.

A number of things combined to bring the Industrial Revolution to America. One was that during the

Perhaps the most important of the many men who helped to bring it about was a shopkeeper-mechanic from Delaware named Oliver Evans.

As a boy Evans learned about the power of steam by filling a gun barrel with water, stoppering it tightly at both ends, and tossing it into the fire. The water boiled to make steam, of course, and the result was a terrific report as the expanding gases popped the plugs out of the barrel. The boy became a wagonmaker's apprentice, and he dreamed of horseless carriages. He connected the idea of steam power with that of the horseless carriage, and he set to work building a steam engine.

Evans dreamed of a high-pressure steam engine. Watt had distrusted high pressure and just used steam to get a vacuum so that atmospheric pressure would force the piston down. Evans was impatient with these sluggish engines. He thought of a closed cylinder with a piston being driven back and forth by high-pressure steam let in at each end and exhausting through valves.

Evans was convinced that this type of engine could drive a steam carriage, but without money to experiment, he discarded the idea for a time and went to work planning America's first automated factory.

Napoleonic Wars, and the War of 1812 trading with England practically came to an end. The goods Americans had become accustomed to had to be made at home. Another was simply that Americans started making steam.

Early efforts were greeted with skepticism, but before long steam brought about a revolution in transportation, as well as in the factory.

In 1825 John Stevens built a locomotive which ran on a circular track around the grounds of his estate at Hoboken, New Jersey.

The inefficient grain mills of the day bothered Evans. Many strong men, he noted, were required to carry grain up the mill stairs in sacks, dump it under the millstone, shovel it into tubs, and haul it up to the loft again where it was "spread with shovels and raked with rakes," and then finally put in barrels.

The water-powered mill Evans built contained no less than five separate inventions, each one of which replaced a man. A conveyor belt with wooden buckets carried the grain to the top of the mill. From there it was automatically moved under the grinding stone, spread and raked, and put into barrels.

The whole operation was automatic, and Evans' idea forms the basis for modern manufacturing techniques. Nobody thought much of the idea at the time. Many years later, though, Evans discovered that his devices were being widely used by settlers in the West who did not bother to pay him for the rights to his inventions.

The mill was a financial failure, but finally, in 1804, Evans received

The very first railway charter in America was granted to John Stevens in 1815.

America's first railroad locomotive, the famous Tom Thumb, *was built by Peter Cooper (right), a skilled mechanic, in 1830.*

the commission that he had long waited for, a steam engine that would clean and dredge docks. Evans built the machine sixteen miles upriver from Philadelphia and decided to run it into town under its own steam. He installed a drive belt, wheels, and a stern paddle, fired up the boiler, and sent the fifteen-ton monster lumbering down the bumpy roads towards the Schuylkill River.

His "Orukter Amphibolos," or amphibious dredger, splashed into the Schuylkill, and Evans hitched the drive belt to a stern paddle. Steaming up the river, he brought the iron monster out of the water in Philadelphia's Center Square water works. Spectators gathered to look at the strange sight, and some ran away frightened, but Evans proceeded calmly with the dredging for which

his engine was expressly designed.

Because of its impassable forests, America relied on water transportation and pioneered the development of the steamboat. John Fitch, one of the greatest tinkerers America has ever known, was the first man to succeed in making a steamboat. "Poor John Fitch" people came to call him, and indeed nothing he did seemed to turn out very well. Even the greatest benefactors of American invention, Franklin and Washington, turned Fitch down when he asked for help.

A passenger on the first run of the De Witt Clinton *in 1831 called the locomotive "a singular looking affair" and the carriages "equally singular looking appendages."*

In Europe a few experiments had been made earlier with steamboats, but the most extensive and successful work began in the United States shortly after the Revolution. Steamboat development seems to have begun with William Henry of Lancaster, Pennsylvania. Henry had been to Europe and came home with dreams of steamboats which he passed on to John Fitch, among others.

In 1787 Fitch demonstrated a steamboat, powered by an engine he had developed with a watchmaker named Henry Voight, to the members of the Constitutional Convention in Philadelphia.

On Fitch's first boat the engine was used to power two sets of paddles, one on each side of the boat. It worked, but not very well, and the members of the convention failed to provide him with badly needed financial support. Fitch added a stern paddle to later versions. His third boat, the *Perseverance*, went eight miles per hour, and Fitch ran it more than 2,000 passenger-paying miles on the Delaware in 1790, seventeen years before Robert Fulton's *Clermont* made its first run up the Hudson.

But Fitch's bad luck held to the end. The *Perseverance* lost money, partly because it competed with the best coach lines in the United States, partly because the engine took up so

In 1807 Robert Fulton's steamboat the Clermont *sailed up the Hudson from New York to Albany. Many people called the startling new vessel "Fulton's Folly."*

much room that there was little left for paying passengers. A year later a storm yanked the boat loose from its moorings and grounded it, and Fitch was too poor to salvage it.

Luckier than Fitch was a courtly Marylander named James Rumsey, who built a steamboat patterned on the jet principle advocated by Franklin.

Backed by Franklin and Washington, he achieved considerable fame and distinction. His boats, however, were less successful, though one of them ran quite well in London, after his death in 1792.

Theoretically, the jet steamboat was fine. Just as Newton said, every action has an equal and opposite re-

action, and by squirting a jet of water out the back end Rumsey's boats went forward. Practical jet engines, however, whether shooting out water or hot gases, were not developed until the middle of the twentieth century.

Two men were finally to share the credit for building and operating successful steamboats. One was John Stevens, a wealthy New Yorker. Stevens had seen one of Fitch's boats perform and— it almost goes without saying—had turned down his plea for help.

Stevens dreamed of establishing a steamboat line on the Hudson River and he very nearly succeeded. In 1807 his *Phoenix* became the first steamboat to go out to sea.

On this plan, Fulton drew himself at the periscope of the Nautilus, *a new submarine he designed for the French in 1801.*

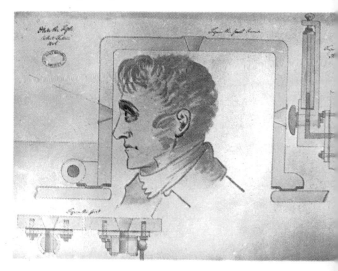

Samuel Slater

Richard Arkwright

Robert Fulton is the other man usually given credit for inventing the steamboat, but he actually did his most imaginative work on submarine design. He had gone to Europe in the early 1800's to study painting but soon turned his hand to invention. His *Nautilus* was the first undersea ship to incorporate many features of the modern submarine. With French backing, Fulton chased British men-of-war around the English Channel with his submarine for several years.

In Paris Fulton met Stevens' brother-in-law, Robert Livingston, who was the American Minister to France. Livingston had tinkered with steamboats himself and suggested they join forces to develop a boat for the Hudson River run. Fulton went to work at once, and soon one of his little steamboats was paddling its way up and down the Seine at four miles per hour.

Fulton then returned to the United States where he went to work on a bigger boat. In 1807, just as Stevens' *Phoenix* was being readied for the trip up to Albany, Fulton beat him to the punch. His *North River Steamboat*, popularly called the *Clermont*, huffed up the Hudson all the way to Albany as spectators lining the shore cheered.

People still asked "what good is it?" and called the *Clermont*, "Fulton's Folly." Fulton made them eat their words. He improved his boat and built more, and he made money from the start, not only because his boats worked well, but because his route lay between two great cities connected on land only by long primitive roads.

Altogether Fulton built twenty-one steamboats, including the first double-ended steam ferry and the first steam warship. He was not, as he frankly admitted, *the* inventor of the steamboat. The *Clermont* used a Watt engine, and some thirty other steamboats had taken to the water before her. But more than anyone else, Fulton encouraged the great era of steamboat travel.

Shortly after Fulton's *Clermont* steamed proudly up and down the Hudson, Stevens' *Phoenix* paddled out to the open sea and down to the Delaware River where she proved to be a huge success.

Stevens and his son Robert L. Stevens then started thinking about putting steam engines on wheels at a time when most Americans were more interested in river and canal transportation. The English had been building steam carriages and even crude locomotives for some years, and Stevens adopted many of their innovations. In 1825 he built a locomotive which ran on a circular track around his summer estate in Hoboken, New Jersey. At the same time his son was devising hardware that would be necessary for rail travel: the T-rail, the wooden cross-tie and the railroad spike.

But Stevens was beaten again, in a way, for the first locomotive made and used by a railroad in the United States was Peter Cooper's *Tom Thumb*, built for the Baltimore and

Arkwright made use of his invention, the spinning frame, in his English textile mills. Samuel Slater, a former Arkwright employee, came to America in 1789. Here he built this Arkwright frame from memory for use in his mills in Pawtucket, Rhode Island.

The Industrial Revolution brought large numbers of textile mills to New England. This machinery was used for spinning and winding cotton yarn on bobbins.

Ohio in 1830. Cooper had been a brewer, brickmaker, grocer, and a glue and iron manufacturer, but he was mostly a mechanic.

The *Tom Thumb* was a brilliant tinkerer's catchall. Cooper simply took a steam engine, stuck it on a wheeled platform, and hitched the pistons to the wheels with a couple of musket barrels. The ingenious little contraption worked, and Cooper puffed impressively around Baltimore with more than thirty passengers in tow.

It was Stevens, however, who took out the nation's first railway charter, and in 1832, at the age of eighty-three, he put the Camden and Amboy railroad into operation in New Jersey.

Railroad tracks—most of them built with iron rails imported from England—soon crisscrossed the East and South. Then, about 1840, the railroad crossed the Mississippi.

In that year America began to roll its own steel rails, and less than thirty years later they were to link the Atlantic and Pacific oceans. Gradually the steam locomotive became a familiar sight to a nation of pioneers moving westward.

Soon the United States began to look west for its materials rather than east towards England. The Western wheat-growing regions came into direct competition with the agricultural industry of the East, but the East was becoming industrial as well as agricultural. Trains and steamboats brought raw materials to the factories that were springing up all over New England.

By this time the factory system had arrived in America. It came across the sea in the form of European invention and technology. This did not happen all at once, of course, but if it had a beginning it was when a twenty-one-year-old British textile worker posing as an English seaman arrived in Philadelphia in 1789, the year George Washington became President of the United States.

Samuel Slater had been apprenticed in England to Jedediah Strutt. Strutt was a partner of Richard Arkwright, who was England's foremost inventor of machinery for textile mills. Because of his association with Arkwright, Strutt was familiar with the most advanced textile machinery in England—and so was his apprentice, Samuel Slater. When Slater's apprenticeship was over, he decided to emigrate to America. Fearful of having his luggage searched by vigilant British customs officers who were guarding British inventions, he memrized the details of the British spinning machines and sailed under an assumed name.

When he reached America he wrote for a job to Moses Brown, a famous and foresighted Quaker merchant whose mills were then turning out cotton goods sadly inferior to those made in England. "I have had oversight," he reported modestly in support of his cause, "of Sir Richard Arkwright's works."

The most notable of America's early contributions to the Industrial Revolution was Eli Whitney's cotton gin. The model at left is one of several that Whitney made when applying for a patent. He first applied to Thomas Jefferson, Secretary of State and head of the Patent Office, in 1793.

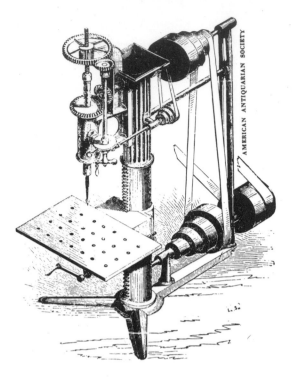

Eli Whitney designed this drill press for his musket factory, where it was used in making interchangeable parts.

For Brown this was a stroke of good luck. "Friend," he wrote back, "we hardly know what to say to thee . . . thou shalt have all the profits made of them (the frame machinery) . . . and this we do for the information thou can give."

When Slater arrived in Providence, Rhode Island, he was appalled by the crude machinery in Brown's shop, and decided he would have to try to build completely new Arkwright machinery. In less than a year, with the help of a good mechanic, he completed the task. First his spinning and weaving machines were powered by a treadmill, but soon Slater had hooked them up to water mills and later to steam. The factory system had arrived.

In 1789, the year Slater arrived in America, a Connecticut Yankee named Eli Whitney enrolled at Yale College. As it turned out, Eli Whitney had almost as great an effect on the industralization of America as Samuel Slater.

In 1793, his years of study over, Whitney left New Haven for Georgia to take a tutoring job. At that time, two kinds of cotton were being grown in the South. One was Sea Island cotton, which grew only along the coast. Its long fibers were loosely attached to slippery black seeds. The other kind was upland cotton, whose sticky green seeds were attached to short cotton fibers.

Sea Island cotton could be separated from its seeds by running it through a roller frame something like an old-fashioned clothes wringer. This machine was called an "engine," or, in the South, simply a "gin." But upland cotton could be separated only by picking out the sticky green seeds by hand.

It was to pick the green seeds from the upland cotton that Whitney invented his famous cotton gin. It consisted of a cylinder with a set of toothed discs something like circular saws. These discs grabbed the cotton and pulled it through slots wide enough for the fibers but too narrow for the seeds. At the same time, a revolving brush removed the cotton from the discs.

Whitney got a patent on his machine in 1794 and began to sell his invention, but with little success. Southern planters had broken into his workshop and examined the machine. It was so simple that they had no trouble copying it, and they built their own gins without paying a cent to Whitney. It took Whitney years to make a profit on his invention.

But the simple little device had an enormous effect on the South. Before the gin, with no cash crop to work on, slaves were becoming impractical and unpopular in the United States. Then Whitney's cotton gin made cotton growing so profitable that within two years the price of slaves doubled, and the amount of cotton exported from the South rose from 138,000 to 1,601,-000 pounds. Much to his chagrin, the Yankee from Connecticut had caused the "rebirth" of slavery.

Disillusioned and downhearted, Whitney returned to New Haven. There he seized upon an idea which had an even greater effect than the gin upon his nation's history. The idea was to produce interchangeable parts so that the lock of a gun, for example, could be made which would fit all other guns of the same type.

The Frenchman Blanc had had the notion first, as Jefferson observed, and in 1798, when the government gave Whitney a contract to make 10,000 muskets, the United States Army at Springfield, Massachusetts, was already engaged in the development of machinery to make interchangeable parts.

Whitney designed his own machines to accurately cut wood and metal, and he developed methods of comparing the measurements of the parts produced.

More than fifty years later some of Whitney's muskets were put on display in London. Even then British officers were amazed at the idea of interchangeable parts, and resolved to adopt the "American System."

By 1847, a young man named Samuel Colt had carried this production system to its logical conclusion. Colt had invented a gun with a revolving chamber. For the first time a man could fire and fire again without reloading. Colt's "equalizer" helped to win the West.

Perhaps even more important than the gun was the production system Colt installed in his factories. He described it this way: "Each workman would receive two or three important parts and would affix them together and pass them on to the next who would add a part and pass the growing article to another who would do the same . . . until the complete arm is put together." Today we call this an assembly line.

In Whitney's factories a man might take the interchangeable parts and put them all together himself. Colt added the assembly line, where each worker performs only one or two operations.

Cyrus McCormick's reaper helped to bring the Industrial Revolution to the farm. The demonstration (above) took place in Vir-

ginia's Shenandoah Valley in 1831. The machine was able to cut six times as much grain per day as could a man with a scythe.

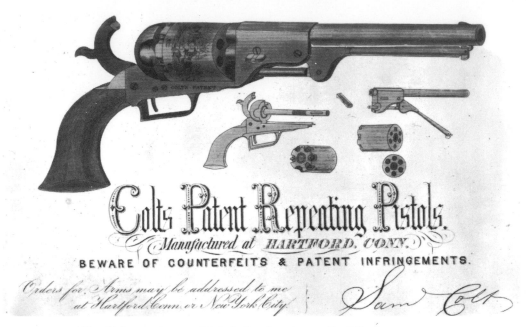

The Colt revolver, which helped to tame the West, was mass-produced from interchangeable parts, on an assembly line.

Steamboats, locomotives, interchangeable parts, the assembly line —the Industrial Revolution in America gathered momentum and rolled west to the prairies.

For years America had to import wheat. In 1831, when Virginia-born Cyrus McCormick built a reaper, he began an agricultural revolution which would reverse this situation. While not actually the first reaper, it was to be the first to meet the challenge of the vast midwestern prairie farms. For years McCormick struggled unsuccessfully to sell his reapers. They would cut more grain than many men with scythes, but farmers never had enough money to buy the machines until the harvest was over—and then they did not want them. Moreover, his machine

was at first inferior to that developed by Obed Hussey of Ohio.

Then McCormick moved out to Chicago, the heart of the new farm belt and there he borrowed a trick from the Yankee peddler. He sold his machines on the installment plan —buy now, pay later. In 1851 he sold 1,000 reapers, six years later more than 23,000. The Great Plains became America's breadbasket.

The settlers moving west also faced the problem of how to fence in their livestock. It seemed like a simple problem, and as it turned out it had a simple solution, but not until 1874 did anyone patent an invention with which to do it. The problem was new in a way: New England had stone for walls, and the South, rich in timber, had rail fences. But

This is the first length of double-strand barbed wire made by Joseph Glidden.

in the West one hundred years ago fences often cost more than the land and livestock they enclosed.

In desperation they tried growing fences of hedge or making "mud" fences of sod. Nothing worked. Nothing, that is, until Joseph Glidden, improving on an idea developed by a man named Henry Rose, came up with something he called "barbed wire." Cattle had walked right through ordinary wire, but the barbed wire was an immediate success. Within a few years millions of miles of it had been strung.

Not long before this the people moving west to farm had faced another problem: the rich soil of the prairies, lacking in stone and grit, stuck like glue to the iron plows they brought with them from the East. The pioneers had been slow to change from a wood plow to an iron one (it would poison the soil, some believed) and they were slow to solve their new problem.

Then in 1837, a young Illinois blacksmith named John Deere suddenly wondered if steel would scour itself when pulled through the earth. He made a steel plow out of an old circular saw blade and gave it a try.

The soil curled cleanly away from the blade, furrow after furrow. As it slid through the earth its vibration caused a humming sound, and people called it the "singing plow."

It is quite possible that Deere's saw blade was made out of British steel, for the making of steel had not kept pace with the booming American iron industry. America had been slow to pioneer in metal production, although the son of a French Huguenot immigrant, Apollos De Revoire, had established a large copper-making factory. Revoire's son—he was called, in the American fashion, Paul Revere—became quite well known in his

Deere's steel-bladed plow was designed to cut through the prairie's clay soil.

57

The first locomotives of the American Industrial Revolution were built here, at the

West Point Foundry. The ironworks began operation in 1818 at Cold Spring, New York.

Sir Henry Bessemer

Alexander Holley

other guises: "Indian" in the Boston Tea Party, despatch rider during the Revolution, and silversmith. And by the first part of the nineteenth century his copper was coating the bottoms of American ships and sheathing the boilers Robert Fulton put on his first successful steamboats.

But steel was a different matter. England had always made it, and America had always imported it.

Even in England, steelmaking was a slow, costly process until 1854, when Henry Bessemer discovered a way to make it cheaply and abundantly. Basically, steel differs from iron only in its carbon content, and Bessemer found that air blown through molten iron would combine with the carbon and other impurities and come out in the form of burning gases.

When Bessemer tried to patent his process in this country, however, he found that a Kentuckian, William Kelly, claimed to have discovered the process independently. The conflict was settled within a few years. Alexander Holley purchased the American rights and, at Troy, New York, erected the first important Bessemer steel plant in the United States.

American invention was picking up, too. In 1857 Americans took out 2,910 patents, a third more than Great Britain took out that year.

This inventiveness had made the country an exporter of steel and wheat. Before the Industrial Revolution most farmers could raise enough food to feed just two families—their own and one other. After the mechanization of agriculture one farmer could feed a dozen families. Factories, steamboats, and railroads spread across the land, and farmhands, who were replaced by machines, left the land and went to work in factories.

There was more ahead of Americans than they could imagine, and many of the Industrial Revolution's developments would become old-fashioned in the years to come. In the field of transportation even the mighty steam engine was to be replaced by something fired by oil, a remarkable new invention: the internal combustion engine.

This drawing shows the giant Bessemer converters of a Pittsburgh, Pennsylvania, steel mill in operation around 1855.

INTERNAL COMBUSTION

The Indians collected oil by skimming surface pools with blankets and wringing them out. They believed that it had medicinal properties, so they gulped it down happily, spread it over their bodies, and mixed it with their war paint. Because it burned, they thought it divine, and the places where it was found they called sacred ground.

The white man called the sour-smelling stuff "Seneca oil," after the Indian tribe. It was promoted as a quack medicine cure-all, but one whiff was enough to upset a weak stomach. Moreover, the oil was a nuisance, fouling the brine wells Americans drilled to get salt. But the stuff did burn, and whale oil for the country's lamps was getting more and more expensive.

It was the kind of opportunity that Americans rarely missed. Men began devising lamps which would burn Seneca oil without making too much stench. One of them was Samuel Kier, a Pittsburgh druggist. Kier also bottled petroleum—as it came to be called—as a medicine. "1849—Wonderful Medical Virtues Discovered," the label on the bottle read.

Wonderful medical virtues or not, tasting Seneca oil was worse than smelling it, and people did not take to drinking it. But the picture on the label of a Seneca oil bottle of a salt-drilling derrick and the words "discovered in boring for salt water" intrigued an ex-journalist named George Bissell. In 1854 he took a bottle of Kier's oil to the country's leading chemist, Benjamin Silliman, Jr., of Yale.

Silliman experimented with the distillation of crude oil, breaking it down into the oils, gases, waxes, and tars of which it is a mixture, and described it as a raw material from which "they may manufacture very valuable products." This professorial enthusiasm turned out to be something of an understatement.

Bissell formed a company and sent men to Titusville, Pennsylvania, to drill for oil with a salt-drilling derrick like the ones used by Kier. The men went down to the salt-well level and found lots of water but no oil. They kept on drilling, though, and in the summer of 1859, a black liquid began to ooze up their pipe. They had struck oil.

Overnight, it seemed, the discovery flashed across the country. Men began drilling for oil everywhere, in fields, pastures, even in their back yards. Titusville and other Pennsylvania hamlets boomed, and shanty-towns grew up around a forest of rickety wooden oil rigs that sprouted

In 1865, six years after America's first well was drilled, an oil company dedicated the Petroleum Court Dance to the "Ladies of the United States."

Several Americans made ingenious contributions to its development. One of them, Alfred Drake, exhibited a gas engine at the Crystal Palace exposition in New York in 1850. But the credit for the first useful gas engine goes to a Belgian, Jean Joseph Etienne Lenoir.

Lenoir's engine, which appeared on the market in France and the

like weeds over western Pennsylvania. Before long the profitable business of Yankee whaling was doomed, and kerosene lamps, using refined petroleum, soon appeared in every American home. But the chief use for oil was still to come.

It came partly because the steam engine had so many drawbacks. It needed a big boiler, and it had to get up a head of steam before it provided any power. All through the age of steam, men had been tinkering with machines which would get rid of the boiler by burning the fuel in the engine itself. These first took the form of gas engines, which burned the city gas that had been available since 1800.

Six years after Drake's well began producing, John Benninghoff's farm near Titusville was covered with oil rigs.

United States in 1860, incorporated many of the basic features of the modern internal combustion engine. It mixed air and city gas in a closed cylinder, ignited the mixture with a spark, and used the resulting expansion of the gases to push a piston—just as expanding steam pushed a piston back and forth in the steam engine. Not long afterwards a German engineer, Nikolaus Otto, built a much more efficient engine which would run on half as much illuminating gas as Lenoir's.

But these early engines had one big drawback: they depended on city gas, and those who attempted to adapt them for vehicles found that they had to carry a complete gas plant along with them. Fortunately, however, gas could also be generated from liquid fuels. Alfred Drake's engine, according to a contemporary report, would also operate on "lard combined with a small portion of whiskey."

Then when oil was discovered a more portable fuel turned up in

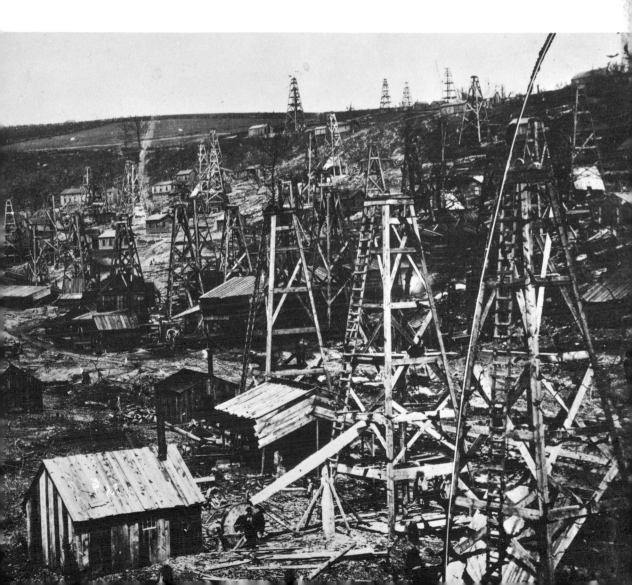

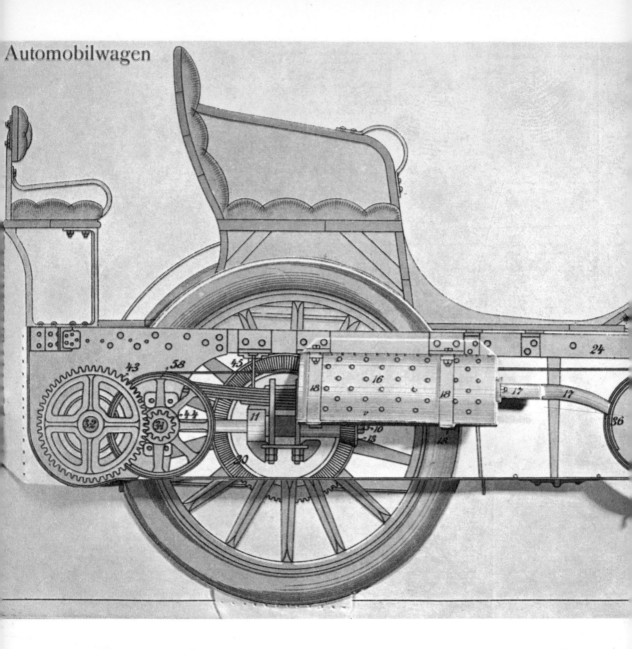

Automobilwagen

Silliman's distillation. This was gasoline, an explosive liquid which was originally considered a waste product. (It was kerosene, another derivative of oil, which people used in their lamps.)

Using gasoline, two other Germans went to work on Otto's invention with the idea of hitching it to a "carriage." Both managed to make

lighter engines than Lenoir's by replacing his single large cylinder with several small ones arranged along a crankshaft.

First they attached the engines to bicycles and made motorcycles, and then they put them on four-wheeled carriages. By 1886 Karl Benz and Gottlieb Daimler were snorting around German streets in their

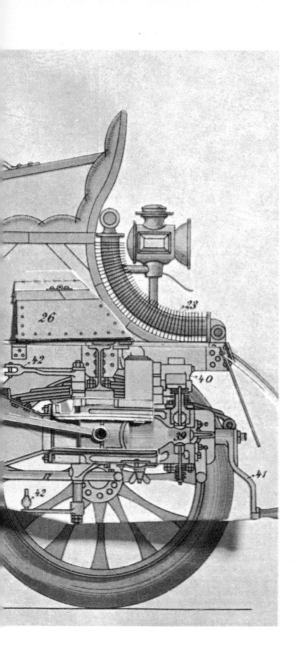

which scored a hit at the Philadelphia Centennial Exposition in 1876.

There it caught the eye of a mechanical-minded patent lawyer named George Baldwin Selden. In 1879, four years before Benz and Daimler started building vehicles powered by gasoline engines, Selden had applied for the first patent on a "road locomotive" with an internal combustion engine (modeled on Brayton's design).

Selden knew that he was way ahead of his time. Roads in America were little better than they had been one hundred years before. So he kept his patent alive by filing amendments to it and patiently waiting for the age of the automobile to arrive.

And arrive it did. Eli Whitney Blake, Whitney's nephew, invented a crusher that would grind up rock to surface roads. Highways were being built, for the European-invented bicycle had become the rage, and Americans clamored for better roads to cycle on. Then the English Dunlop invented the air-filled pneumatic bicycle tire to cushion the jolts on bad roads.

As a result, cars of all kinds began to appear on roads in Europe and the United States. Some, like the famous Stanley Steamer, were still powered by steam.

When battery-powered electrics

horseless vehicles. Both set up automobile companies which later merged. Today their famous Mercedes is still considered one of the finest cars in the world.

Still another useful fuel, which we now call diesel oil, was to be found in distilled petroleum. George Brayton, an Englishman living in Boston, built an oil-powered engine

Henry Ford is pictured in the first car he built, the 1896 Quadricycle.

became popular, a New York journalist predicted happily that city streets would become "almost as quiet as a country lane—all the crash of horses' hoofs and rumble of steel tires will be gone."

But by the turn of the century gasoline engines were becoming the most popular. The "rumble of steel tires" was gone by this time, but the report of the backfire and the angry voice of slapping pistons were heard through the land. Internal combus-

tion engines were noisy, and they had a dirty, smelly exhaust, but still, you did not have to recharge the battery every night and you did not have to fire up the boiler if you wanted to keep going.

Then somebody had another idea. Why not mass-produce cheap cars? Instead of making them by hand they could be put together on an assembly line, in the same way Samuel Colt had made guns. The idea was conceived by Ransom E. Olds, who launched his Oldsmobile factory in Detroit in 1899. His runabout was steered by a tiller, and it was tiny compared to the elegant French cars of the day, but for several years Olds was enormously successful with his "merry Oldsmobile." In 1905 Olds turned out 6,500 cars. Then, for some strange reason, his business backers made him give up the idea of making light, cheap cars in large numbers and go back to making heavier, more expensive ones.

A man named Henry Ford took up the idea, but before Ford could start mass-producing automobiles he had a fight on his hands. For in 1899 a group of businessmen had gotten together in an attempt to corner the automobile market. Nobody (or so they thought) had bothered to take out a patent on the liquid-fueled automobile, and they figured they could easily buy up the patents for the various parts their cars would need. Then they came across George Selden's patent, which was still being renewed.

Selden turned out to be less of a stumbling block than they expected. He sold out when he was offered handsome royalty payments, and the company then seemed to have a complete monopoly on manufacturing automobiles with gasoline engines. They grandly offered the privilege of making cars to others— for a good stiff price—and the automobile manufacturers figured there was nothing else they could do but pay. By 1906, more than 1,000 of the country's 1,500-odd automobile dealers refused to sell unlicensed machines. One by one the gasoline automobile manufacturers came to terms with the situation.

But not Henry Ford. "Tell Selden to take his patent and go to hell with it," he said, and started to fight the monopoly in court. The legal battle dragged on for eight years. Ford won in 1911, when the court ruled that Selden's patent applied only to cars using the Brayton engine.

In the meantime Ford had been making cars in spite of the monopoly. But like Olds, Ford had another battle on his hands convincing his backers that they should mass-produce cheap cars. They felt that he should build cars almost by hand the way the old French carriage makers were doing it.

Ford did not agree. He wanted a simple, rugged, cheap car.

The answer was the Model T, first produced in 1909. Ford put the interchangeable parts of his car on a moving assembly line. Each man added a part, and the assembly lines came together at the end to form the final product. By 1913 a thousand cars a day were rolling off the line. Two years later the one-millionth Model T chugged out of his Detroit factory.

Ford finally sold 15,000,000 almost identical Model T's before he was forced to change the design in 1927. The cars were the same be-

69

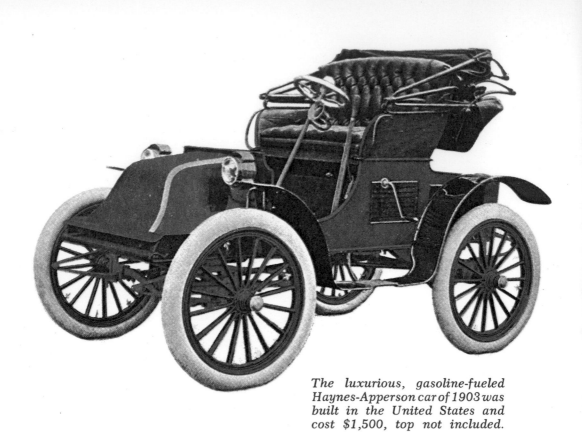

The luxurious, gasoline-fueled Haynes-Apperson car of 1903 was built in the United States and cost $1,500, top not included.

Charles Duryea was photographed in 1898 (below) driving one of his own automobiles. Charles and his brother Frank built America's first gasoline car in 1893.

Daimler's first four-wheeled, gasoline automobile appeared in Germany in 1886.

The Stanley Steamer (above) was invented in 1897. Its builders powered the engine with steam rather than gasoline.

cause he thought that if he "froze" his design, keeping it the same year after year, he would be able to lower their price from time to time. And he was right. The price of the Model T dropped from $950 in 1909 to $290 in 1926.

Finally Ford had to change the Model T to compete with other companies like Chevrolet which began introducing new gimmicks and styling changes on its cars every year. American taste was changing.

The internal combustion gasoline engine also revolutionized life on the farm. For many years, steam engines had been used to pull and power threshing machines, and a man named Richard Jordan Gatling, whose machine gun had been adopted by the Union at the end of the Civil

War, had invented a steam plow.

These plows and tractors were huge steam-belching monsters which ran on enormous iron wheels. On some models a stoker had to run alongside shoveling coal into the firebox, and the weight of the ma-

The Columbia Electric Surrey was built in 1900. It was nearly noiseless, since it was powered by two storage batteries.

chine on its heavy wide wheels packed the ground so hard it could hardly be plowed.

C. H. Parr and C. W. Hart built some of the first gasoline tractors at their plant in Iowa in the early 1900's. In 1903 Benjamin Holt added the endless track, or caterpillar tread, to tractors. It made it much easier for them to climb around on really rough ground, and gave rise to the bulldozer and the modern tank.

In that same year two brothers, who ran a bicycle shop in Dayton, Ohio, were also making history. Orville and Wilbur Wright were not unlike the early American clockmakers who turned to invention and used their mechanical skill to put machines together. The machine the Wrights had in mind was the airplane.

Man had dreamed of flying for centuries. The first successful manned flight was the Montgolfier balloon ascent that Franklin watched with such interest in 1783. A year later a Frenchman and his American patron, Dr. John Jeffries, tried a flight across the Channel from England to France. Halfway across, the balloon lost most of its lifting power, and the desperate aviators had to throw everything overboard, including most of their clothes. Thus lightened, the balloon rose, and they bumped to a safe—if nearly naked—landing in France.

Soon man wanted to steer these lighter-than-air contraptions which floated about with the wind. An Austrian suggested using trained eagles; but the eagles did not co-operate. Airscrews, or propellers as they came to be called, turned by manpower, were tried. They were not effective enough to counter a strong wind, even when the gasbag was streamlined into a cigar shape. And steam engines were certainly much too heavy.

Eventually man turned to the gasoline engine. The perfected dirigible, or steerable balloon, with a gas engine to spin its props, was the work of the German Count Ferdinand von Zeppelin. During the first World War the German Navy used his zeppelins for bombing and scouting, and afterwards they started transatlantic air travel.

But the zeppelins were clumsy and slow, and their gasbags were filled with highly inflammable hydrogen gas which had an unfortunate way of catching fire. When the German airship *Hindenburg* blew up at Lakehurst, New Jersey, in 1937, the whole idea was very nearly abandoned.

In the meantime, serious work was being done on heavier-than-air ships, but the problems were much harder to solve. One of the first serious efforts was made by Hiram Maxim. In 1894 he built a magnificent multi-

In 1775 Blanchard and Jeffries crossed the English Channel — traveling from Dover to France — in a winged balloon.

winged contraption driven by a huge, 360-horsepower steam engine. It was really nothing more than a powered box kite, but Maxim put it on guide rails designed to hold it down on its test run, got up steam, and whisked it down the track. So powerful was the engine that Maxim's craft broke through the restraining rails and started to rise.

At this point the startled Maxim stood an excellent chance of being the first man to take off in a heavier-than-air machine. It may have occurred to him that the honor would come posthumously, for he had no way to control the machine in the air. So the inventor cut the power, the multiplane crashed, and the unnerved Maxim went back to his work on automobiles, lightbulbs, mousetraps, and machine guns and never tried to fly again.

Not long afterwards another American, Samuel Pierpont Langley, started to work on the problems of flight. Langley was more scientist than tinkerer, and when he became secretary of the famous Smithsonian Institution in 1887, he began a serious study of what was then known about the science of flight.

Langley built a series of model aircraft powered by steam engines which he called "aerodromes." In 1896 one of them soared nearly a mile over the Potomac River in a highly successful flight. Since all that Langley had wanted was proof that flight was possible, he was ready

to drop the project, but President McKinley and the War Department appropriated $50,000 and urged him to build a man-carrying machine.

In 1903 Langley assembled a full-scale "aerodrome" on the roof of a houseboat on the Potomac. Langley's mechanic, C. M. Manly, calmly climbed into the cockpit, and the craft was launched, but it fouled its catapult device and flopped into the river. The salvaged aerodrome was launched again with Langley at the controls, and splashed into the Potomac a second time. He had come close to success, but the newspapers made cruel fun of him, and Congress told the Army not to waste any more money on flying machines.

At the time, however, everyone thought it was a failure.

In Ohio an Episcopalian bishop might well have shaken his head and said, "I told you so." Bishop Wright had once dismissed men's attempts at flying with these words: "Men will never fly, because flying is reserved for angels." But the bishop's words were apparently wasted on his sons Wilbur and Orville. They had been thinking about flying machines from the time they were boys. Although they had no formal educa-

On October 7, 1903, Dr. Samuel Langley tried to fly his "aerodrome" or airplane. The top picture shows the plane mounted on a catapult on top of a houseboat in the Potomac River. The second picture shows the plane leaving the catapult. At bottom, the airplane has crashed.

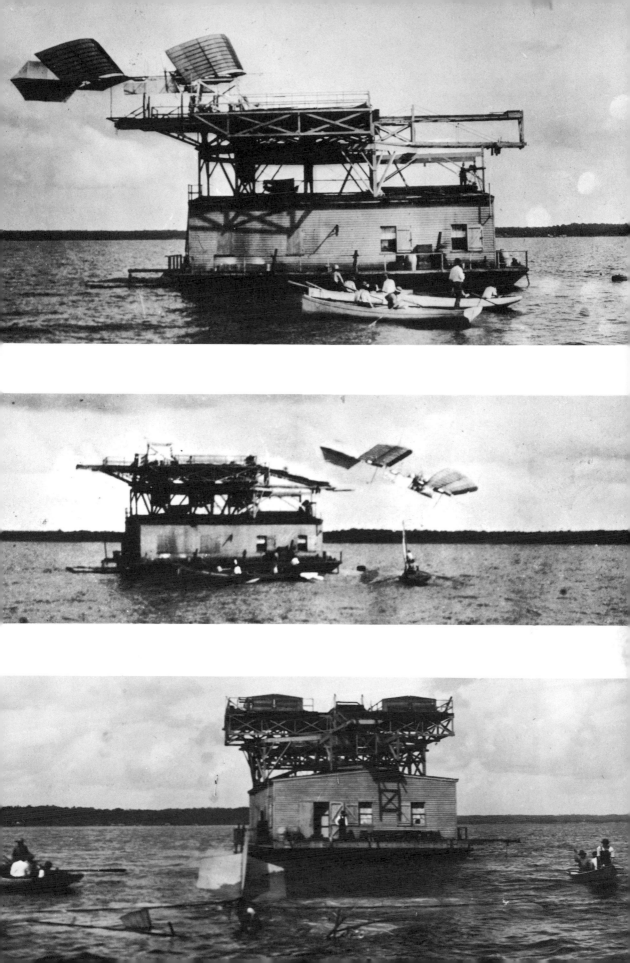

tion, they read everything they could on the subject.

The real problem facing the Wright brothers was not propulsion —the light gasoline engine solved that; nor a wing surface that would provide lift—Langley and others had overcome that difficulty. What nobody had done so far was to devise a way to steer a plane in the air.

With the help of a wind tunnel which they built out of an old starch box, and after many experimental glider flights, they discovered that their machine should have a tail, and that they could provide control over the plane by twisting the tips of the wings. Ropes stretching from the pilot's "cradle" to the wing edges "warped" them to give one wing

The Wright brothers built this glider (above) in 1901. Their gliders taught them how to control a heavier-than-air craft in flight. On December 17, 1903, the Wright brothers' airplane (at right), powered by a twelve-horsepower engine, took off at Kitty Hawk, North Carolina, with Orville Wright at the controls.

more lift and the other less, just as birds do with their wing muscles.

On the sand dunes at Kitty Hawk, North Carolina, in December of 1903, just nine days after Langley took his dousing in the Potomac, the Wrights were ready to give it a try. It was a bitter windy day, and the "biting cold made work difficult," Orville jotted down in his diary.

Sand whistled along the dunes as the brothers laid down a track for the take-off truck the plane rested on.

With the engine already roaring, Orville squirmed through the struts into the lie-down cradle, flipped the lever that released the brakes, and the plane lurched forwards. Soon Wilbur, who was alongside holding onto a wing tip, was trotting and

Orville (left) and Wilbur Wright

straight up. The French built one as early as 1907, a crude flimsy affair which employed the basic principles of the helicopter. The wing was thinned down to the size of a "blade" and spun around on top of the plane. The early helicopters proved unstable, however, tipping over and crashing after rising a few feet.

The first practical helicopter was designed by a Russian named Igor Sikorsky. He had built the first four-motored airplanes in Russia before the first World War, and when he emigrated to the United States he attacked the problem of the helicopter.

His solution was an ingenious device which caused the spinning blades to change their angle of pitch as they went around the rotor shaft. In 1942 Sikorsky's company delivered its first helicopter to the Army Air Force for use in World War II.

It was not until after World War I that aviation really came into its own in the United States. The nation was thrilled when Charles Lindbergh, the "Lone Eagle," spanned the Atlantic nonstop, when Jimmy Doolittle set one of his speed records, and when Richard E. Byrd became the first man to fly over the North and South Poles. America watched in awe and admiration as

then running full tilt. Just as he almost fell he let go. The plane rose, flew for almost 200 feet, then nosed down, and slid to a stop on the sand.

The Wright brothers made four flights that day. The longest lasted 59 seconds and covered 852 feet. That night a still doubting Bishop Wright received a now-famous telegram: "Successful—four flights on Thursday morning—took off with motors from level ground—average speed thirty miles an hour—longest flight 59 seconds—inform press—home for Christmas—Orville."

As planes grew bigger and heavier they required longer landing fields, and before long man tried to make a machine that would take off her fearless young aviators flew the mail, cracked speed records, crossed the oceans in heavier-than-air machines, and performed unbelievable stunts.

Flying grew up during these years, and the development was international: in Germany, Hugo Junkers developed the all-metal monoplane with thick wings that needed no outside bracing; Ernst Heinkel, Willy Messerschmitt, and the Englishman Frank Whittle developed the first jet aircraft; German draftsmen came up with the idea of the swept wing to make jets faster; an American, James Whitcomb, dreamed up the "coke bottle" fuselage to ease jets through the sound barrier.

Nobody knows what the final version of aircraft will be. It may have no wings; it may be round and flat and saucer-shaped; it may be powered by new chemical fuels or by the atom.

But we do know that it all began with the discovery of oil, with the tinkerers who found out how to harness the explosive power of gasoline in the internal combustion engine, and with courageous men like the Wright brothers who put together the flying flivvers that first put man up with the angels.

Charles A. Lindbergh, the first man to fly alone across the Atlantic, is seen here with his plane, the Spirit of St. Louis.

THE ELECTRICAL REVOLUTION

Less than a decade after Benjamin Franklin died, Joseph Henry, a boy of Scottish ancestry, was born in Albany, New York. His parents were poor, he had little education, and at an early age Henry thought he wanted to be an actor and a playwright.

Kept indoors one day with a minor ailment, he became interested in science by reading an English book on astronomy and chemistry. He decided to devote himself to "the study of nature," and the results were impressive. By the time he was forty, he had invented the modern electro-

magnet, discovered the principle of induction upon which generators and electric motors are based, devised a telegraph system, and had done some of the research that was to lead to the invention of transformers and to the development of wireless telegraphy.

Yet today Henry's name is unknown to many Americans. Unlike Franklin, he had a European rival of equal ability, Michael Faraday, who was working on the same problems—and received the lion's share of the credit for solving them.

The two men were studying the connection, which everybody believed to exist, between electricity and magnetism. Both men were familiar with the electromagnets invented by the Englishman William Sturgeon in 1825. Sturgeon had insulated a horseshoe-shaped iron bar by varnishing it and had wound a coil of bare copper wire around it. When current was sent through the wire, the iron bar became a magnet.

Henry improved on Sturgeon's electromagnets by insulating the wire itself (at first he wrapped it in silk ribbons from his wife's petticoats) and winding it several layers deep around the iron bar. In this fashion he finally made one that would lift 3,600 pounds. Today's giant electromagnets work on the same principle.

In 1831 Faraday announced to the Royal Society that he had discovered the principle of induction. In one of his experiments he had moved a bar magnet in and out of a hollow coil of insulated wire, and a current was in-

81

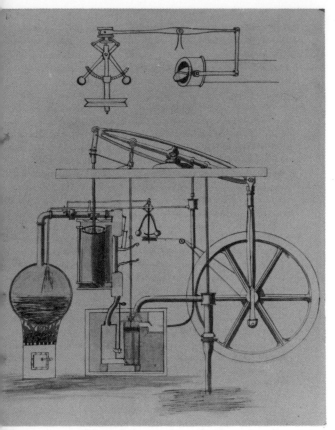

A student in Joseph Henry's chemistry lectures at Princeton around 1845 made these sketches of laboratory apparatus.

duced in the wire while the magnet was in motion. "Thus is obtained," a fellow scientist wrote, "the result so long sought after—the conversion of magnetism into electricity."

In another experiment Faraday placed two wires side by side, but not in contact, and passed a current through one of them. A current was momentarily produced by induction, in the other wire in the opposite direction. This was the fundamental scientific discovery in the series which was to lead to electric generators and motors.

Henry had performed similar experiments and reached much the same conclusions, but he had published nothing. When he read Faraday's paper he quickly wrote up his own findings and showed that his work, whether earlier or not, had gone more deeply into the subject. He also described "self-induction," an "extra" current which appears in a coil of wire when its connections are broken.

With a knowledge of electricity second to none, Henry casually put together equipment for his own convenience that was to lead to inventions later credited to other men. For instance, he set up the first telegraph in this country, in 1831, stringing almost a mile of wire around and across the classroom where he taught in Albany, New York.

At one end was a sending device or transmitter, hooked up to a battery (invented by the Italian Alessandro Volta around 1799), to send pulses of electric current through the wire. At the other end was an iron bar wrapped in the wire. When an electrical impulse came through, the bar, now magnetized, repulsed one end of a permanent magnet set on a pivot. The other end swung away from the magnet and clanged a small office bell. This was the first electromagnetic telegraph.

Henry was lured away from his research in 1845. An Englishman, James Smithson, had given the United States more than £ 100,000 to "found at Washington, under the name of the Smithsonian Institution, an establishment for the increase and diffusion of knowledge."

Congress chose Henry as the first Secretary of the Institution. There he was able to continue some of his work, but he never again had the time to investigate nature with his early zeal and devotion.

The choice was a wise one for many reasons. For years, Henry ably directed the course of American science and gave invaluable aid to many an American inventor. Some of them became far more famous than Henry himself—Samuel Finley Breese Morse, for example.

Before he took to invention Morse had been an artist—and a good one. After graduating from Yale, he had studied painting for twenty years, and in 1832 was considered one of America's foremost painters.

Then, on the way back from a three-year period of study in Europe aboard the packet ship *Sully*, Morse decided that he wanted to be an inventor. By the time he got off the boat he had made sketches of a device he called the telegraph.

Morse knew almost nothing about electricity, but he was convinced that Americans could make anything they put their minds to, and he began playing around with batteries, wire, and iron bars. As he disembarked from the ship he remarked casually to the captain: "Should you hear of the telegraph one of these days as the wonder of the world, remember that the discovery was made on board the good ship *Sully*."

Morse was less confident after he made his first pathetic attempts at telegraphing. He could not even get a current to flow through his rig until a chemist showed him how to insulate his wire and wind it properly around the horseshoe-shaped iron bars. Finally, he improvised a primitive apparatus in which the magnetism induced in an iron bar would pull a pen down on a strip of moving paper to make dots and dashes.

But the instrument would only send a signal over a short distance, so Morse went down to Princeton, New Jersey, to talk to Joseph Henry. Henry, of course, had long since built a telegraph, and in Princeton he even had one set up between his home and his laboratory. He was more interested in research than in exploiting the commercial possibilities of telegraphy, so he patiently explained to Morse what was wrong with his system, and how to "relay" a signal over long distances without any loss of power. Henry's relay—he had invented it six years before Morse came to see him—was simply a device with its own electrical-power source which would boost a weak signal along as it came through the circuit.

With Henry's help, and that of his assistant Alfred Vail, Morse had a practical telegraph line ready by 1843. Using broken bottle tops for

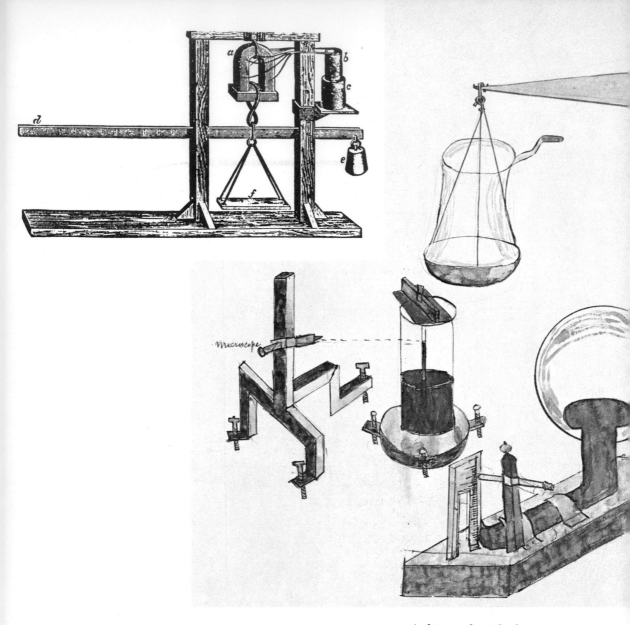

As his work with electromagnetic induction advanced, Henry built stronger, bigger electromagnets. His sketch for an electromagnet (top) shows an experimental set-up in which a horseshoe magnet (a) has been wound with insulated wire and electrified by the battery (bc). Henry eventually built an electromagnet that was capable of lifting tons of metal. Henry also built these experimental induction coils (left). Joseph Henry probably set up the equipment (above) for physics experiments he performed for his class in Natural Philosophy. A student made the sketches.

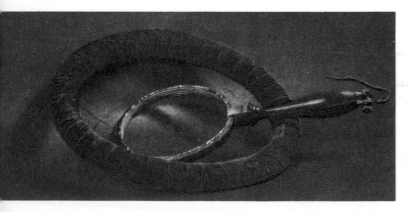

insulators, the wire was strung from trees and poles between Washington and Baltimore. Morse sent the first message from the Supreme Court room in the Capitol to Vail in Baltimore: "What hath God wrought?"

Morse's system was not actually the first to go into commercial operation. Sir Charles Wheatstone already had one in England, but it did not produce an audible signal, and Morse's method of signaling soon took the place of all rival forms of the telegraph.

Morse's telegraph owed more than he would admit to Henry's advice and to Alfred Vail's invention of portions of the system. But it was Morse who exhibited the determination and persistence needed to sell a new device to an indifferent public.

When he died in 1872 his telegraph covered the globe with a cobweb of wires strung from poles, underground, and even under the sea.

Morse had experimented with submarine telegraph cables and he was vice president of the New York, Newfoundland and London Telegraph Company, founded by Cyrus West Field. The company's objective was to string a line under the Atlantic.

Most of the money and all of the cable for the job came from England, but Field was the project's driving force. The United States and British navies each lent a warship to carry and unroll the cable, and they began to lay it in 1857.

Everything went wrong from the beginning: the cable broke, the insulation sprang a leak, the line stopped carrying signals for no known reason. But in 1858 the cable was at last laid all the way from Ireland to Newfoundland. Queen Victoria sent the first message: "The Queen desires to congratulate the President [Buchanan] upon the successful completion of the great international work in which the Queen has taken the greatest interest."

Just two weeks later, the cable suddenly went dead. Undismayed, Field rounded up more money and obtained the services of the English vessel *Great Eastern*, a huge 22,500-ton experimental passenger liner five times the size of any previous ship. Although she had failed as a passenger liner, the *Great Eastern* was beautifully engineered and built and proved to be a perfect cable-laying ship. After one failure the line was successfully laid in 1866, and from then on telegraphic communication across the Atlantic has never ceased.

The telegraph was a triumphant success, but it was soon to be followed by something even more remarkable. And once again, Joseph Henry played his part.

On a cold rainy day in March, 1873, a man who taught speech to deaf-and-dumb pupils came to the Smithsonian to ask Henry for help. The visitor was a tall young Scot with bushy black hair, side whiskers, and a droopy moustache. Alexander Graham Bell told Henry that he had

been trying to send spoken words over wires.

The problem, Bell said, was to vary the intensity of an electrical pulse in the same way that sound waves vary. Bell, as he wrote to his parents at about that time, was having trouble: "My inexperience in such matters is a great drawback. However, Morse conquered his electrical difficulties although he was only a painter, and I don't intend to give in either."

Nevertheless it was a disheartened Bell who faced Henry in the spring of 1875. Henry encouraged him. "You have the germ of a great invention," he said. "Work at it."

Bell complained: "But I have not got the electrical knowledge necessary."

"Get it!" said Henry.

Bell got it. By that June he was sending musical notes over a wire, and by the next March he could say to his assistant over the wires: "Mr. Watson, please come here. I want you." Unlike Morse, Bell gave Henry full credit. "But for Joseph Henry," he told his friends, "I would never have gone ahead with the telephone."

In May of 1876 President Grant and Emperor Dom Pedro of Brazil opened the Philadelphia Centennial Exposition. A team of invention judges toured the vast Machinery Hall where a mammoth steam engine drove scores of machines.

No one paid much attention to Bell's little telephone exhibit until late on June 25, when the judges, accompanied by Dom Pedro, were about to quit for the day. Dom Pedro recognized Bell when Henry pointed out his little exhibit, for he had met him a few weeks before in Boston. "How do you do, Meester Bell?" said the burly Brazilian, beaming through his beard, "and how are the deaf-mutes in Boston?"

Bell said he was sorry the judges would not inspect his apparatus until the next day, when he had to be back in Boston.

"Ah!" said the emperor, "then we must take a look at it now."

Bell stationed Dom Pedro in a

receiver booth and then went down the hall and talked into his transmitter. "To be or not to be," enunciated Bell with his Scotch burr, "that is the question."

"My God!" said Dom Pedro, "it talks."

But a lot of people called Bell's invention a "humbug," so Bell took the telephone on tour and gave demonstrations in Boston and New York. Gradually people began to see how the telephone could be used, and by the turn of the century more than a million and a half telephones were in use.

Prior to his invention of the telephone, Bell had patented a multiple telegraph which could send several messages over a single wire at the same time. In later years he was to invent or perform research in a number of scientific fields.

He sponsored research on the phonograph which lead to the first disc records, built an early iron lung, devised hydrofoil speedboats powered by airplane engines, and pioneered a number of aviation improvements including the wing-tip aileron, which superseded the Wright brothers' "wing warping" method of control.

Another exhibitor at the Philadelphia Centennial was a cocky,

twenty-nine-year-old named Thomas Alva Edison, who was to become one of the greatest inventors of all time.

Edison had been something of a problem child. His mother had taken him out of school and taught him herself because his teacher reported that he was "addled." His wild experiments drove his parents nearly to distraction, not without good reason. When he was six Edison set a small fire in his father's barn "just to see what would happen." The barn burned down.

Later he set up a laboratory in the cellar of the family's house in Port Huron, Michigan, and his parents became more or less accustomed

Samuel Morse, photographed here by the famous Mathew Brady, gained much of the knowledge which helped him build his telegraph from Joseph Henry. Yet Morse gave Henry far too little credit for it.

This 1846 painting titled War News From Mexico *captures the excitement of Americans who could go to the telegraph office and find out almost instantly what was happening hundreds of miles away in the Mexican War. Before Morse's Lightning Wires went into use, all news dispatches had had to travel slowly overland.*

to the periodic explosions of powders and chemicals that shook the house.

As a youth Edison became a wandering "tramp" telegrapher, skilled but irresponsible. Before long, he began to invent. When he was twenty-two he engineered an improved stock ticker which could keep up with the frenzied speculation then taking place on the New York Stock Market.

When the Western Union Telegraph Company bought out the stock ticker company, their president, General Marshall Lefferts, asked Edison how much they owed him for his inventions. Ready to accept as little as $3,000, Edison asked:

"Well, General, suppose you make me an offer."

"How would $40,000 strike you?" Lefferts inquired.

In 1837 Morse built his revolutionary telegraph "register and port rule," one of the first successful inventions to put electricity to use in communications. The wooden frame (right) holds the electromagnet, at center, and the "register," or receiver itself, on the right side of the frame. The "port rule" or transmitter (above) was cranked by hand. By 1846 Morse had improved his invention and patented the instrument below. This telegraph had the same basic parts the other instruments had, but it could be operated more smoothly and could send and receive over much greater distances.

While returning from Europe on the sailing ship Sully *in 1832, Samuel Morse made these sketches for a telegraph code which would be marked on moving strips of paper.*

telegraph and invented wax wrapping paper and the mimeograph machine. Soon he began taking out a patent a month.

In 1876, the year of the Centennial, Edison built a new laboratory on an estate in Menlo Park, New Jersey, and continued his policy of "inventions to order." One of the first to come from the new shop was an improved telephone transmitter. Bell's device, an iron diaphragm that vibrated to sound waves and caused a similar effect on the electrical pulse, was not powerful enough.

Edison devised a simpler, higher powered mouthpiece which eliminated the need for shouting into the telephone, but this did not occupy him for long.

One day Edison handed one of his assistants a sketch for an apparatus that looked like a small hand-turned lathe. The handle turned a cylinder wrapped in tinfoil, and as it revolved a needle scratched a groove in the foil. When the contraption was built, Edison turned the crank while shouting, *"Mary had a little lamb, whose fleece was white as snow!"* He then put the needle back in the starting position and turned the crank again. A scratchy squeak came out of the machine:

"Mary had a little lamb,

whose fleece was white as snow."

Edison nearly fainted, but he managed to blurt out that it struck him fine.

The electrical engineer, as Edison called himself, set up shop in Newark, New Jersey, where he improved the

Thus was the phonograph born. Unlike most inventions, to which many men contribute, it was a completely new concept. Nothing even remotely like it had even been suggested to the Patent Office, and for once Edison got a patent almost without an argument.

The phonograph, which was built on a budget of eighteen dollars, was just one of more than 1,000 patents Edison took out during his lifetime. Probably the most famous of them all was United States patent number 222,898 for "an Electric Lamp for Giving Light by Incandescence." In other words, a lightbulb.

For years inventors had experimented with electric lights made of platinum wires or carbon rods. In 1877 Charles J. Brush had invented a highly successful carbon "arc" lamp which gave off a brilliant flame. The arc lamps were fine for street lighting, but much too bright for household use. And if the current was cut down, the lamps simply went out instead of dimming.

Edison tried out numerous materials to see if they would carry a current and glow: coconut fibers, lampwick, even hairs from a friend's beard. Finally he tried passing a current through a carbonized thread in a vacuum—and it worked.

In 1836, struggling to simplify his code, Morse made notes (above) on the frequency with which various letters of the alphabet occur in English. The simplified version of his code (below) was completed and ready for use in telegraphy by 1837.

But Edison's first bulb wore out in forty-five hours. "There's a better way to do it . . . find it!" Edison used to say to his assistants, and nobody took the advice more to heart than Edison himself. In a few more months he discovered that a thread of carbonized paper would give several hundred hours of reasonably effective service.

Edison's lamp was not the first incandescent lamp—both Europeans and Americans had invented others before him. But his was the first that

could compete with the gas and oil lighting of the day.

Nor did the "wizard," as he came to be called, stop with the mere bulb. He improved and assembled much of the equipment that makes our modern electric power possible: a

In July, 1886, this fleet set sail from southern Ireland, bound for Newfoundland with the Atlantic telegraph cable. The ships of the fleet were: the Great Eastern, *which carried the 2,500 miles of cable;* H.M.S. Terrible; *the* Albany; *the* Medway; *and the* William Cory. *The fleet reached its destination successfully on July 27, 1866. The telegraph had joined two continents together.*

Alexander Graham Bell is seen making the first telephone call between New York City and Chicago, in 1892, sixteen years after his invention of the first telephone.

generator (considered almost as important an invention as the incandescent bulb), electrical meters, conductors, underground power cables, and, as Edison put it, "a thousand details the world never hears of it." At last the consumer of electricity was freed from reliance on the perishable chemical battery.

In 1882 Edison opened an electric generating station on Pearl Street in New York, and for a time it was one of the wonders of the world.

Edison worked mostly with direct current, that is, a current which flows in one direction only and normally has a low voltage. For certain purposes D. C. current, as it is called, is still the best, but it is almost impossible to send it over long distances. As the low-voltage current passes through a wire it quickly becomes weaker and weaker. Even if larger cables were used to carry a bigger load, power dropped off sharply. This meant that the Edison stations had to remain small and practically in the customer's back yard.

Faced with this difficulty, Europeans were experimenting with a new kind of power. In 1884 their experiments were noted at a fair in Italy by the American George Westinghouse. Westinghouse, the inventor of the air brake which did so much to make railroads a safe way to travel, brought samples of the machinery for A.C.—alternating current—back to this country.

A.C. continually reverses the direction in which it flows. Thanks to the transformer, the device which sprang from Joseph Henry's experiments, the low-voltage A.C. power ordinarily produced by a generator can be "stepped up" to high voltage and sent hundreds of miles over a line without serious loss of power. At the end of the line the dangerous high-voltage current can be stepped down with another transformer for safe household use.

With his associate William Stanley, who perfected the transformer, Westinghouse started building A.C. systems. Edison and his backers fought him tooth and nail. "Just as certain as death," Edison said, "Westinghouse will kill a customer within six months after he puts in a system of any size."

Westinghouse admitted that A.C. would kill people. "So will gunpowder and dynamite and whiskey and lots of other things," he added dryly, "but we have a system whereby the deadly electricity of the alternating current can do no harm unless a man

The telephone operators of 1888 were called "Hello Girls." This photograph was taken in New York City's New Cortlandt exchange, which employed forty women.

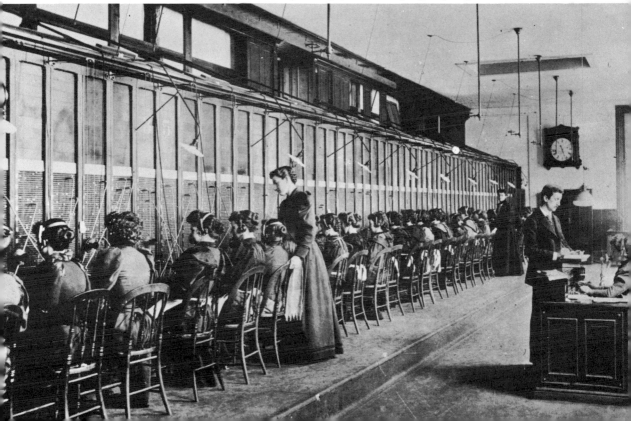

Bell exhibited and demonstrated several telephones at the Philadelphia Exposition of 1876. This receiver was one of those seen by the public.

is fool enough to swallow a whole dynamo."

To dramatize their argument the Edison faction promoted the use of high-voltage A.C. for the execution of criminals. On August 6, 1890, the first victim was "Westinghoused," a word some people were unkind enough to use before the new word electrocuted was widely adopted.

The "war of the currents" raged until 1892-1893 when the Edison company became part of the General Electric Company, and the Westinghouse system was adopted for the gigantic power plant that was to be constructed at Niagara Falls.

While Westinghouse and Edison were battling to see whose system would provide America with electric power, a number of men were at work trying to take the wire out of the telegraph system; to make, in

other words, a "wireless."

It began in 1887 when a German scientist named Heinrich Hertz proved that electric sparks cause vibrations or waves which race through space with the speed of light—186,000 miles per second. The existence of these waves had been suspected by Henry, Faraday, and the British physicist James Clerk Maxwell. But it remained for Hertz to prove it.

A year after Hertz died in 1894, an Italian inventor, Guglielmo Marconi, put together a device with which he hoped to be able to send Hertzian waves through space. Basically it contained three parts: a transmitter invented by Hertz; something called a coherer, invented by the Frenchman Edouard Branly, which could detect Hertzian waves (it was made of little metal particles which would stick together or "co-here" when struck by them); and a radio antenna invented by the Russian, Popov.

At first about all Marconi could do with his rig was to ring a bell fifteen feet away. His father, who could think of easier ways of ringing bells, was not impressed, but Marconi persisted. Finally he built an apparatus that could send the Morse code, and year by year he increased the distance over which he could send messages.

By 1899 Marconi was able to communicate between two battleships thirty-six miles apart, and that same year the invention saved the crew of a ship grounded on the Goodwin Sands off the southeast coast of England. Two years later Marconi, in Newfoundland, picked up three faint dots—the Morse S—sent from one of his stations in England.

Other inventors began to improve the parts of the Marconi radiotelegraph. Reginald Aubrey Fessenden, a big, ruddy, bearded Canadian who had worked for Edison, invented a better receiver than the coherer, an "electrolytic detector" something like the first telephone transmitter. Moreover, it was able to turn the sounds of the human voice into radio waves and reverse the process at the other end.

On Christmas Eve of 1906, Fessenden staged the first radiotelephone broadcast. Owners of Fessenden wireless sets, which had always clicked out the Morse code, were astonished to hear voices and music coming out of their apparatus.

But commercial radio broadcasting and radio telephoning did not become a reality until another device superseded Fessenden's detector. It was called the triode vacuum tube, or audion, and it was the invention of an American scientist named Lee de Forest. The audion, which has been described as one of the greatest

This model shows the kind of telephone transmitter used by Alexander Graham Bell and Dom Pedro of Brazil in 1876.

This is a replica of Edison's first practical incandescent lamp—which he made in his laboratory at Menlo Park in 1879.

inventions of all time, boosted the current—and therefore the strength of the signal—received in radio sets.

For his efforts, de Forest was prosecuted for fraud on the grounds that he was selling stock in a company to make "a strange device like an incandescent lamp . . . which device had proven worthless." But when commercial radio broadcasting began in 1920, it was de Forest's audion that made it possible.

Gradually the science of radio and electronics improved. Marconi found that he could send certain types of radio signals all the way around the world by bouncing them off the "heaviside" layer in the earth's electrified ionosphere (the layer was named after its discoverer, Oliver Heaviside). Frequency-modulation radio, which eliminates the radio static from electrical storms and other causes, was invented by Edwin Armstrong. Hundreds of engineers, working for more than a decade, figured out how to turn light and dark elements of a picture into electrical impulses and then turn them back into an image on a screen. Commercial electronic television (mechanical systems had been in use since about 1920) appeared in the 1930's.

Man had come a long way from the time when Joseph Henry hooked up wire, iron bars, and a battery, and rang a bell in his laboratory in Albany.

Quiet little electric motors replaced steam and gas engines. Trains and streetcars drew smooth silent power from the generating stations of Edison and Westinghouse. Sprawling American cities shot upwards, thanks to the electric elevator which helped to make skyscrapers practical. The smell of oil disappeared from homes, and the flickering light

In 1893 Edison patented the Strip Kinetograph (left), the first movie camera.

Edison had worked seventy-two consecutive hours improving his wax cylinder phonograph when this photograph was made.

99

Thomas Edison spent a lifetime in his laboratory. He was awarded 1,093 patents — more than any other man in American history.

of oil lamps was replaced by the steady glow of the incandescent lamp. American factories discarded their enormous steam engines. Now they could turn on power with the flick of a switch.

When Thomas Alva Edison died in 1931, it was proposed to President Hoover that the nation observe a total blackout for a minute or two, that all power be shut off in homes, streets, and factories. Perhaps only

then did Americans realize what Edison and his inventions really meant, for the suggestion was obviously out-of-the-question. So important was electrical power to the nation that to do without it even for a few minutes would have caused chaos.

So instead, many people simply dimmed their lights in silence, on the day of Edison's funeral, in honor of the man who had done more than anybody else to put the great power of electricity at his countrymen's finger tips.

Lee de Forest, called the "Father of Radio," invented the radio vacuum tube in 1906.

TURN OF THE CENTURY

In 1893 the World's Columbian Exposition opened in Chicago, and Americans had never seen anything quite like it. Architects had designed a "white city" gleaming with plaster of Paris. The buildings and grounds were covered with heroic statues; one, called *The Republic*, was 65 feet high from the hem of her dress to the top of her laurel wreath. Bands played while visitors were pushed around the Fair in rolling wicker chairs or were paddled in gondolas around artificial lakes and pools surrounding the buildings.

Towering over the whole Fair was an enormous Ferris Wheel, 264-feet high, which could carry sixty passengers in each of its thirty-six cars. It had been designed by an engineer, George Washington Gale Ferris, when he was challenged to produce something for the Fair even more impressive than the Eiffel Tower in Paris.

To the young man who had grown up in the rural South and worked his way out to the Exposition selling copies of a book called *What Can a Woman Do?*, it must have been quite a sight. Lee de Forest, then twenty years old, got a job as a chair pusher,

and he had chosen his own favorite spot at the Fair—"When my patrons asked me what they should visit . . . I would steer them into Machinery Hall."

Machinery Hall in Chicago was quite a contrast to the one in Philadelphia in 1876. Gone was the outrageous maze of slapping steam-powered drive belts and the shadowy flicker of oil and gas lamps. Instead, there was the quiet purr of little electric motors and the bright steady glow of electric lights. The hall's electrical equipment ran on an A.C. system devised by George Westinghouse, who was also trying to promote his electric stoves and irons. Thomas Edison was there, too, and Alexander Bell, and hundreds of other American inventors.

The previous decade had been one of the greatest of all time for invention. The automobile, the trolley car, the incandescent light, the cash register, the dynamo, the pneumatic tire, smokeless powder, transparent

Americans first rode the Ferris Wheel at the Columbian Exposition in Chicago in 1893. The wheel – a great engineering achievement in its time – was 264 feet high and carried 2,160 passengers.

THE
FERRIS WHEEL
MIDWAY PLAISANCE
WORLD'S
COLUMBIAN EXPOSITION
· CHICAGO 1893 ·

LINE OF VISION, 258 feet.
POINT OF WHEEL, 264 feet.
R OF WHEEL, (center of pins,) 250 feet.
EIGHT OF WHEEL AND CARS, 2100 tons.

TIME REQUIRED FOR ONE TRIP, 20 minutes.
DUPLICATE REVERSING ENGINES, 1000 horse power each.
TOTAL WEIGHT of wheel, levers and machinery, 4300 tons.

There was a marked speed-up in the pace of American living as the nineteenth century drew to a close. Trolleys run by electricity (such as the 1892 model at right) clanged and rattled through city streets. As urban buildings grew taller, electric elevators replaced "vertical railway cars" (such as the 1881 hydraulic elevator which is shown below).

This ingenious slide fastener, invented by Whitcomb L. Judson in 1891, is the original ancestor of the modern zipper.

film, electrical welding, the steam turbine, the electric furnace—all these important things and many more had come into use in the years since 1880.

Some seemed enormously important. In 1889 Charles M. Hall of Oberlin, Ohio, received patent number 400,665 for the "manufacture of aluminum." Others seemed trivial. In 1893 patent number 504,038 was granted to Whitcomb L. Judson for a "slide fastener." Today we call it a zipper, and billions of them have been manufactured.

Cameras, typewriters, sewing machines, and hundreds of other gadgets were being perfected. Bridges

were being built of steel, and skyscrapers were just around the corner. So were mass-produced automobiles and airplanes. America was riding fast and high.

A few years after the Fair was over, a Japanese commissioner visiting the United States wrote: "We said 'what is it about the United States that makes it such a great nation?' and we investigated and found that it was patents, and *we* will have patents."

At that time the patent system was nothing like the one that Whitney, Evans, and Fulton had struggled under. By an act of Congress in 1836, the patent law was reorganized and improved. The "examination" system which makes it necessary to determine the novelty and usefulness of a patent application was instituted. From then on the patent system was able to regulate the fast pace of American invention, although it often fell behind on getting the paper work done.

But it was not just a fair patent system that was responsible for the flowering of American invention. The real reason was that Americans liked to tinker with machinery, machinery that the United States needed badly for its expansion.

On the other hand, only a handful of natural scientists, men who are content to explore nature for its own sake, had been born in America. Franklin was one, but even he wanted to put nature's secrets to

Most Americans did not much care. After all, were not they ahead of Europe in electric generating stations, in miles of railroad, in steel production? Could not they build bigger bridges, put up taller buildings, and drill deeper holes for oil? Invention certainly seemed to bring more impressive results than pure science could bring.

There was one man who cared deeply about scientific research for its own sake, a man whose work on physics and thermodynamics could equal Europe's best. Josiah Wil-

practical use in inventions. Count Rumford was the same way. Joseph Henry was an exception. He was a true researcher as opposed to an inventor, and his work on electricity helped inventors the world over in many ways. But in the United States he received much less recognition than he would have received had he worked in Europe.

Most of the theoretical work was being done in Europe, and the machines that were revolutionizing life in the United States were based on this European learning.

This 1882 advertisement suggests that the sewing machine—patented by Elias Howe in 1846—was becoming a fixture in the homes of American newlyweds.

lard Gibbs was born in 1839 and died in 1903, ten years after the Columbian Exposition; and he provided the scientific world with a bridge between the old mechanical world of Isaac Newton and the new relativistic world of Albert Einstein.

The brilliant Clerk Maxwell, then considered perhaps the greatest physicist in the world, once reported that thanks to Professor Willard Gibbs of Yale College, "problems which have long resisted the efforts of myself and others may be solved at once."

It is not easy to explain what Gibbs did. So advanced was his work that the great scientist once sadly noted, after thirty years of teaching at Yale, that only about half a dozen of his students had profited from his courses. Gibbs may have underestimated himself here, for although many failed to understand what he was talking about, they were nevertheless inspired by his teaching. Lee de Forest wrote this tribute in his diary: "I can fervently say that it was Willard Gibbs's influence and inspiration which so firmly resolved me to prepare myself for that project in research and invention which I had determined should be my life's work."

Still, Newton's mechanical system was much easier to understand. He had opened the eyes of the world to a universe that moved in an orderly mechanical way—like the parts of a watch. By paying close attention to the rules he laid down, men could design machines that worked efficiently —and discard the plans for those that would not.

Gibbs went one step further. He studied the borderland between physics and chemistry, where the changes which occurred could not be seen or counted. Out of it he developed his "phase rule," a keystone in thermodynamics.

But Gibbs work was also to have practical results. His "phase rule" alone has resulted in hundreds of practical applications. It has guided metallurgists to the production of new alloys and explained the effects of heat on the properties of metals; it unravelled the constitutuion of portland cement and standarized its method of construction.

Still, there was only one Gibbs, and Europeans, who looked down on American science just as they had looked down on American manufacturing in colonial times, wondered how such a great thinker could have been born in this country. For the United States was a world of multiplying machines and mass invention, they thought, and not a world of science.

To a large extent they were right. Even in the latter half of the nineteenth century the genius of Americans was in tinkering, in putting machines together with their hands, in selling large numbers of the machines they mass-produced. They were still, in a sense, Yankee clockmakers—ingenious, clever, industrious, and not very scientific.

This dynamo, known as the "Long-waisted Mary Ann," was built by Edison to supply power for the experimental system of electric lights he set up at Menlo Park, New Jersey. When it began operating in 1879, it was the most efficient generator that had ever been made.

On September 4, 1882, Edison's electric light company opened the Pearl Street Power Station to supply Manhattan's first electric light district. The picture (above) shows its thirty-ton "jumbo dynamos" in operation.

"Inventions to order," Edison advertised, and that was to be the blueprint for American science and invention until today. Edison's shops were to be the forerunners of great industrial laboratories where "teams" of scientists would tackle difficult problems and come up with the answers.

As the nineteenth century ended, the machines that science was making possible were becoming too complicated for any one man to develop. Automation, for example, would take many men, working many years, before it became practical. Only a few years after the first television broadcasts it would take tens of thousands of men working together to engineer something which would be called an atom bomb.

Some thought the day of the individual tinkerer, like Whitney, or of the inventor and his mechanic, like Morse and Vail, was fast coming to a close. Scientists and inventors would be harnessed into research teams in industrial laboratories.

Yet there were many exceptions. Simple things could still be invented at home. Charles F. Kettering could

OVERLEAF: In 1875, New York City had no skyscrapers, automobiles, or electric lights. Fulton St. and Broadway were lit by gas lamps and choked with horse-drawn vehicles. Thirty-six years later (see page 118) a modern city had risen.

still putter around in the attic of the family barn and come up with the automobile self-starter.

And even today the individual inventor is not yet extinct. He continues to invent. Bakelite plastic, the diesel engine, and television are a few inventions from old-fashioned lone inventors. And the industrial research laboratory is scorned by some scientists who prefer to take a post teaching and researching in a university. They look down on the teams of scientists who, they feel, are using science and not truly advancing it.

But it did not always turn out that way. In fact the second American to win a Nobel Prize in chemistry received it for original work in the

General Electric Laboratories in Schenectady, New York. Young Irving Langmuir joined the laboratory in 1909, and he had strong reservations about a place which was organized for the purpose of turning out inventions the public would buy. It sounded too commercial, and he thought that he would probably be put to work on some routine job which would have as its sole purpose the making of money for General Electric.

To his surprise, the director of the laboratory told him to look around and decide what sort of research he would like to do. "When I joined the laboratory," Langmuir said later, "I found there was more 'academic freedom' than I had ever encountered in any university."

The result was that Langmuir stayed at the General Electric Laboratory for more than fifty years, and Americans have much for which to thank him. He developed the modern tungsten filament lamp which gave off white light instead of yellow. Everybody thought the way to make a better lightbulb was to get a more perfect vacuum inside it, but Langmuir took just the opposite tack —he filled his bulbs with gas.

It had to be a gas that would not combine chemically with the filament and destroy it, as oxygen combines with iron to produce rust. Ni-

Seen here in his laboratory at General Electric is Irving Langmuir. Here he invented the modern gas-filled lightbulb.

trogen gas turned out to be the answer to the problem.

Then Langmuir went to work on de Forest's audion and perfected vacuum tubes for hundreds of different electrical uses. He received his Nobel Prize for fundamental discoveries in chemistry and, in 1945, led the research team that first produced rain artificially by seeding clouds.

America was growing up along with huge companies like General Electric, Westinghouse, and Bell Telephone. Products put together with machine-made interchangeable parts rolled off assembly lines and into American homes in huge numbers. To make things go even more efficiently in the factories, and to significantly increase production, a practice called scientific management was instituted.

It was founded by Frederick Winslow Taylor, an aggressive little man who talked, people said, faster than a machine gun. Taylor had started at the bottom of the booming steel industry and worked up to chief engineer and general manager of a steel company. After several years of work as a consulting engineer, Taylor retired in 1901, and spent the rest of his life preaching the gospel of scientific management.

Taylor's idea was to speed up the assembly line and enable workers to do a bit more. First he studied the movements a worker made in doing his job, then he arranged the man's work and tools so that they could be handled with the least moving around and reaching. By getting rid of waste motion, the worker's output could be increased without making his job more tiring. The factories where his system was used were known as "Taylorized" plants.

Taylor also put many other aspects of factory management on a scientific basis. He developed standard methods for lubricating machines, systems for keeping track of borrowed tools, and so on.

Taylor's systems met with plenty of opposition. Some came from factory managers who did not want their old system upset. Even more came from workers who feared they would somehow be cheated by the

new methods. Gradually, however, Taylor's system grew to be accepted by factory managers and workers.

When he died in 1915 Taylor left several able disciples. One of the most famous was Frank B. Gilbreth,

In 1883 the greatest engineering marvel of the age—the Brooklyn Bridge—was opened with a burst of fireworks. John Roebling, relying on the power of steel cable, had designed the world's longest span stretching 1,595 feet over the East River. Roebling died before the bridge was finished, and his son carried on his work.

There is much complicated wiring inside modern data processing machines. Scientists today have developed these electronic "brains" to the point where they are now capable of taking over jobs formerly done by humans.

whose children, Frank, Jr. and Ernestine, recorded his adventures in the popular book, *Cheaper by the Dozen*. Gilbreth applied the principles of scientific management to his home life. He discovered that it was faster to button up a vest from the bottom rather than from the top. When one of his children had appendicitis, he set up a kind of human assembly line and sent all twelve of his children under the doctor's knife. It saved time and money to do it that way, he said, since all the children would probably have to have their appendix taken out sooner or later anyway.

To squeeze seventeen extra seconds out of his day Gilbreth lathered his face with two shaving brushes, one in each hand. He also tried shaving with two razors at once, but here his efficiency program broke down. He lost more time bandaging cuts than he saved by shaving both sides of his face at the same time.

But many of his timesaving short cuts became standard operating procedure in factories across the United States.

Today, a new science called automation is doing its best to get man out of the factory altogether. Oliver Evans pioneered automation back in 1782 when he created automated grain mills which required only one man instead of five to operate the machinery.

Today a couple of men can run a pipeline operation or an oil refinery or a simple manufacturing operation. Instrument panels, computers, and television screens tell the operators how work is going in all parts of the plant. If something goes wrong a red light flashes on a control panel telling them what has happened and where. Still, it will take man, who has been called the most efficient computer of all, to fix this elegant machinery when it has unavoidable mechanical or electronic breakdowns.

This sort of advanced technology did not spring full-blown from "Yankee inventiveness." It was a long, hard pull from the rather primitive electrical machinery of the turn of the century to today's modern factory equipment, and it was work that required the most highly trained scientific minds, not just mechanical ability.

That there was still a long, hard road ahead did not occur to many visitors to the Columbian Exposition.

It looked to them as though Americans had invented just about everything there was to invent. True, it was fifty years earlier that the story went the rounds about the man from the Patent Office who resigned because there was nothing left to invent, and a lot of things had come along since then. But in 1893 there seemed again to be little future for the Patent Office.

Steam, gas, and electricity had all been tamed and put to work for man in machines. The mysterious, silent power of electricity was changing the country and the world, and it seemed as if Americans had reached the end of their search for perfection.

But unknowingly man stood on the threshold of a new age. Only a handful of people had heard about certain work being done in Europe; it had something to do with waves, particles, and atoms, and it was hard to see how anything practical could come of it.

As a matter of fact, the scientists themselves had no idea where this research would lead them, and the results of some of their experiments were so astonishing that they could not even believe each other. Some British physicists thought their legs were being pulled when, in 1897, J. J. Thomson reported his incredible notion that atoms were divisible, and that "negatively charged particles can be torn from them by the action of electrical forces." As it turned out, it was no joke.

In 1911, when this painting of lower Manhattan was made, America's scientific and engineering skills had made New York City a wonder-

land of skyscrapers, bridges, and machines. The age of the ocean
liner, the electric light, and the automobile was here to stay.

THE ATOM

Nearly five centuries before the birth of Christ a Greek philosopher coined the word *atomos* from the Greek words *a* (not) and *temnein* (to cut).

Democritus thought that matter—all the things we see and touch—was composed of combinations of tiny solid particles called atoms. His idea was advanced without any experimental evidence; but centuries later Newton adopted it as part of his explanation of the world.

"It seems probable to me," Newton wrote, "that God in the beginning formed matter in solid . . . hard . . . particles . . . even so very hard as never to wear or break in pieces; no ordinary power being able to divide what God himself made one in the first Creation."

No one has yet seen an atom, for our most powerful microscopes cannot see it, but this idea of the "solid" and indivisible atom lasted for nearly 300 years. In 1897 the atom was still intact, although a number of people had begun to suspect that something peculiar was going on inside this tiny particle. The people who worked with electricity had come especially close to guessing some of its secrets. Franklin's experiments had convinced him that electricity was composed of "subtile particles" which could easily penetrate metal. Edison had observed the same particles in action jumping between the negatively and positively charged filaments in his lamps, and an American physicist, Henry Rowland, finally proved that electric currents were simply electrically charged bodies in motion.

But what were these electrically charged bodies? The British physicist, Stoney, thinking that they were just a kind of atom with an electrical charge on it, called them "electrons." Several scientists devised a sort of "bottle" in which the electrical atoms could be generated. The Crookes tube, as it was called after its British inventor, was simply a

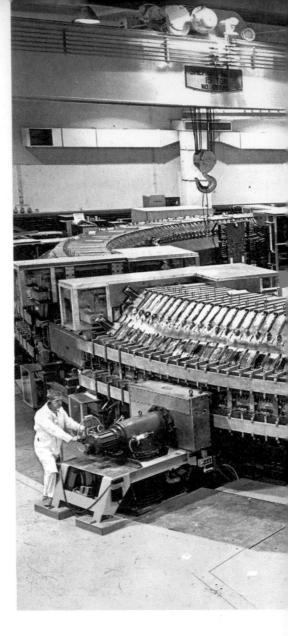

glass tube that could be hooked up to the positive and negative terminals of a battery. When the air was pumped out of the bottle, scientists found that a current would flow through it. The flow of charged particles was called a "cathode ray."

Then in 1895, a German physicist Wilhelm Konrad Roentgen, discovered that a surprising thing happened when these cathode rays smashed into solid matter. The collision produced a new kind of ray which would pass right through opaque substances. Roentgen called it the "X" (for unknown) ray. Physicians were delighted with the new ray which would throw a shadow of the bones within human flesh on a photographic plate. With it they could look right into the human body without cutting it open.

The cathode and X-radiations were soon joined by another, called radioactivity (although it has nothing to do with radio). This is a radiation given off spontaneously by a few minerals such as uranium, without the need of any electric current. A Frenchman, Henri Becquerel, discovered it when he noticed that some photographic plates were exposed after having been left in a drawer with uranium.

In 1897 J. J. Thomson published his paper on cathode rays. In it he announced that the cathode ray was composed of negatively charged particles much smaller than the atom. These particles were electrons. It was soon realized they came from the atom—divisible after all!

It was hard to believe. Ever since the atomic theory of the Greeks had been revived the atom had been thought to be the smallest possible particle. Now Thomson said that much smaller particles existed of a

definite size and carrying an electric charge. Not only that, but some rays were partially composed of these all-but-unknown particles.

But Thomson's work with the negatively charged electron needed further proof. It was supplied in 1911 by an American scientist, R. A. Millikan, who measured the electric charge on the electron.

He did it with a relatively simple apparatus consisting of two charged plates enclosing a drop of oil. By changing the charge on the plates Millikan was able to watch the oil droplets holding electrons float up or dive down as the charge was varied. By studying how they behaved he was able to estimate their mass and the strength of the electrical charge they carried.

Millikan's ingenious oil drop experiment brought him a Nobel Prize in 1923.

Sir Joseph J. Thomson, a great English scientist, was one of the founders of modern experiments in atomic physics.

Meanwhile one of Thomson's students, the New Zealander, Ernest Rutherford, began exploring the uranium atom. Studying the radiation discovered by Becquerel, Rutherford found that two different kinds of ray were involved. Then a third ray was found in radium, the element discovered by the Curies. These three rays were named after the first letters in the Greek alphabet, alpha, beta and gamma.

Rutherford found that the alpha ray was made up of a stream of particles identical to the atoms of the gas helium, minus two electrons. The beta ray was a stream of electrons. Gamma rays turned out to be X-rays; and so the study of radioactivity was shown to be connected with the study of electricity!

Radioactive substances such as uranium and radium shoot these particles out in a constant stream. Thus the substances lose both mass and energy in the process and "decay" into something else. Over a period of 1,580 years, scientists figured, half of a chunk of radium would disintegrate into lead. Thus not only was the atom composed of smaller particles, but it could also change. That was the first hint that the atom could be split.

Rutherford went on to show that the atom contained a center, or nucleus, containing particles called protons. The proton, he found, weighs 1,838 times as much as an electron. Rutherford also found that the atom is enormously spacious. If the nucleus is thought to be the size of a marble, then the tiny electron would be more than the length of an entire football field away.

As the scientists looked into the atom, which they had actually never seen, it occurred to them that it was not unlike the solar system with its small planets wheeling endlessly around a central sun.

An American, Ernest Orlando Lawrence, gave them an even better idea. He developed an atomic "firing range" in which he could shoot particles at high speeds into the atoms of various substances. By studying the impact of the atomic bullets —electrons or protons—scientists could, in a sense, see the insides of the target atoms.

The machine, called a cyclotron, was the first of a whole family of particle accelerators. Today's models can fire particles at nearly the speed of light, 186,000 miles per second, and many of them work on the same principle as Lawrence's first cyclotron. Lawrence used powerful electromagnets to swing his charged particles faster and faster around a circular tunnel. Finally they were allowed to run off through a narrow slit and crash into the target atoms.

His first cyclotron started firing in 1932. That turned out to be quite a year for the United States in more ways than one. The country was in the middle of the depression, and millions of workers were unemployed. Franklin D. Roosevelt was elected President of the United States, and in Germany a man named Adolf Hitler came to power. Fearful of Hitler's dreams of conquest, many European scientists began emigrating to the United States. One of the first was Albert Einstein, who had made the statement in 1905 that energy can be changed into matter, and matter into energy.

Einstein's formula for the conversion was $E = mc^2$, where E is energy, m is mass, and c is the velocity of light, 186,326 miles per second. What the formula really meant was that if atoms could ever be pried apart the tremendous forces holding their nuclei together would be released in the form of energy. To find out how much, multiply the mass

Niels Bohr made important contributions to the understanding of atomic structure.

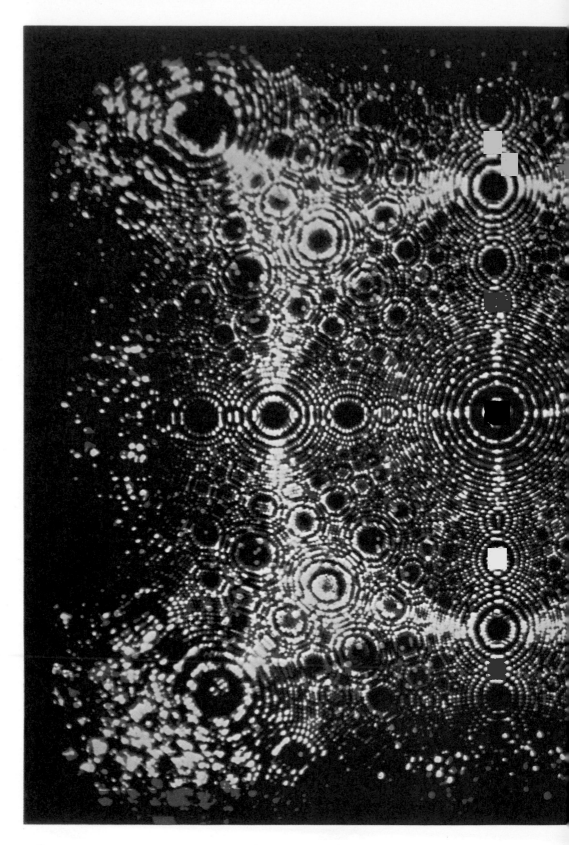

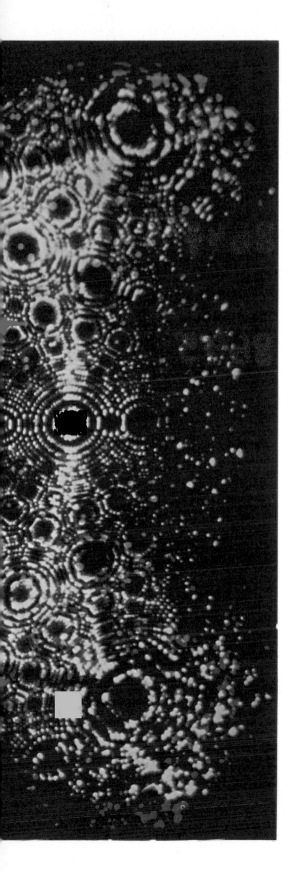

being destroyed by the speed of light *squared*, quite a lot of energy no matter what units you express it in.

Then in 1932, still another particle was discovered in the nucleus of the atom. From his laboratory at Cambridge University, James Chadwick announced his discovery of the neutron. It was heavy, and it had no charge at all. Physicists soon realized that here was a fine shell to fire into atoms.

Electrons and protons were good bullets, but they had one disadvantage. Since like charges repel each other, both tended to shy away from other electrons and protons in the target atoms. Neutrons, on the other hand, would not be repelled or deflected from direct hits on the nucleus of an atom, and soon scientists all over the world were shooting neutron projectiles into uranium atoms: Otto Hahn, Lise Meitner, and Fritz Strassmann in Germany; Enrico Fermi in Italy; Leo Szilard in Hungary. Gradually it became apparent that the atom was actually splitting during the collisions that took place.

Albert Einstein, who knew so well the relationship between energy and matter, soon realized what the new discoveries meant. Alarmed by Hitler's activities in Europe, and urged

The countless atoms in a single crystal at the tip of a platinum needle are seen here magnified 750,000 times. In order to stop movement of the atoms, the needle had to be cooled almost to absolute zero, which is minus 459.69° Fahrenheit.

on by other scientists, he sent a letter to President Roosevelt in August of 1939: "Some recent work by E. Fermi and L. Szilard . . . leads me to expect that the element uranium may be turned into a new and important source of energy in the immediate future . . . [and] would also lead to the construction of bombs."

What Einstein had in mind was a chain reaction among the atoms of a radioactive substance, one that would keep firing off neutron bullets as it decayed. These bullets would crash into neighboring atoms, and then, maybe, two neutrons would fly off, and the next time four, and so on, almost infinitely until the enormous energy locked up in matter would be freed in one split-second breaking apart.

There was, in fact, a material that would give off from one to three neutrons when hit by a single bullet. Fermi and Szilard had shown it to be a rare uranium. If enough of it could be brought together and held together for just a tiny fraction of a second, the mass would become "critical," a chain reaction would start, the huge forces of the atom would be unlocked, and its enormous energy would be available to man.

At first Einstein's warning was ignored, but spurred on by the thought that Hitler might get the bomb first, America finally agreed to try and make one. This decision was made on a fateful December 6, 1941, just one day before Pearl Harbor, and the top secret Manhattan Project came into being.

As Hitler terrorized Europe, more and more scientists emigrated to America. Never in the history of the world had so many top physicists gathered in one country: from Italy, Fermi and Emilio Segrè, who would win his Nobel Prize in 1959; Niels Bohr from Denmark; Einstein, of course, from Germany; Edward Teller, later called the "Father of the H-bomb," John van Neumann, one of the greatest mathematicians of recent times, Leo Szilard, and Eugene Wigner from Hungary. All of them made invaluable contributions to the Manhattan Project.

One by one the scientists filtered into the country—not without difficulty in some cases. The British had to smuggle Niels Bohr out of Sweden in the bomb bay of a Liberator bomber.

Under the utmost secrecy, the men went to work on the Manhattan Project. Their job was to make a "topic boat," a code name for the atomic bomb. There were two approaches to the bomb: one group wanted to fuel it with Uranium 235 (the number stands for the total number of protons and neutrons in the nucleus of the heavy metal), the other with plutonium.

At Columbia, Charles Dunham and other scientists figured out how to separate the precious U-235 from ordinary U-238 which occurs abundantly in nature. To produce plutonium, Enrico Fermi, under the code name, Eugene Farmer, directed a team of scientists at the University of Chicago. Their job was to build an atomic "pile" which, it was hoped, would produce plutonium during a controlled chain reaction.

Fermi, Wigner, and others went to work in an abandoned squash court under the basement of Stagg Field at the University of Chicago. The pile, or reactor, was quite simple in conception. It was built out of blocks of pure graphite (the "lead" in our pencil) and other graphite blocks

containing little pellets of uranium. The uranium would give off neutrons, and the graphite would slow them down so that they would collide with other uranium nuclei at just the right splitting speed. In case a chain reaction got out of hand, cadmium rods were to be inserted into the pile. They would absorb neutrons and stop a runaway reaction.

As soon as the graphite blocks started going into place, the whole squash court turned into a slippery black hole. Scientists wearing goggles slithered around the floor, building up their pile like children with blocks of wood. Finally, on December 2, 1942, Fermi was ready. He ordered all the control rods pulled

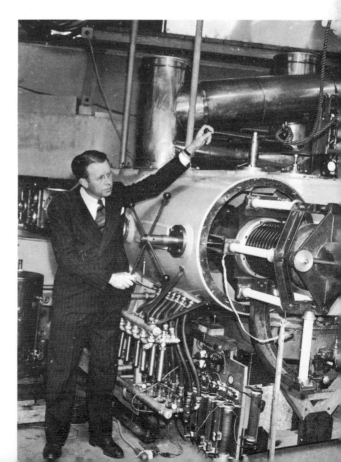

E. O. Lawrence, the cyclotron's inventor, seen at the controls of an atom smasher.

out save one which he noted calmly to those present, "is sufficient to prevent a chain reaction."

Then, little by little, the last control rod was pulled out. Geiger-Müller counters, invented by Geiger and Müller in Germany, started to click, the group of spectators became more and more tense. By noon the reactor was producing large numbers of neutrons, but it had still not gone critical.

At 3:20 that afternoon Fermi gave the final order: "Pull it out another foot." Nervously the three-man "suicide squad" perched on top of the reactor readied their equipment. If anything went wrong, they were to try to douse the atomic fire with a solution of cadmium. Slowly the last control rod was inched out the final foot.

The radiation level shot up, and a chain reaction started in the pile. For the first time in history, man was splitting the atom and getting predictable heat and energy from it.

From Chicago, from Columbia University on the East Coast, from the University of California on the West, American and European scientists filtered out to a secret location among the canyons of New Mexico known to them only as Site Y.

There were scientists from all over the world. Nobody knew what this collection of brains was doing in the middle of the American desert except, perhaps, the Russians. One of the most brilliant people there, sci-

entists recall, was a German-born British citizen named Klaus Fuchs. In 1950, Fuchs confessed that he was spying for the Russians the entire time he was working at Los Alamos, the real location of Site Y.

In Hanford, Washington, giant reactors were constructed to breed plutonium. In Oak Ridge, Tennessee, an atomic city then called "Dogpatch" was built to separate U-235 from ordinary uranium by Dunham's gaseous diffusion process. Atomic bomb fuel from both places were trucked to Site Y. Under the laboratory direction of Robert Oppenheimer, the scientists went to work figuring out how to contain a critical mass of the material in the giant atomic bomb which they were building.

Early in July, 1945, the top scientists began to leave Los Alamos. Late in the evening of the sixteenth, some of the men returned, dog-tired, dusty, dried out. Fermi was so exhausted he went to bed without a word.

That morning, in the Alamogordo Desert, these men had set off the first atomic bomb. It was not announced at the time, but it had been a nerve-racking experience. A thunderstorm had come up, and lightning played across the desert. Dr. Robert Bacher of Cornell had trouble arming the bomb (the desert heat had made the core expand so that it did not fit properly), and all but a few of the men were ordered out of the area.

In 1957 this atomic explosion occurred during tests on the Nevada desert.

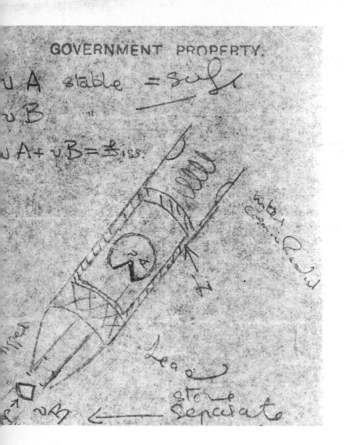

Serving his jail sentence in England after giving atom secrets to the Russians, Klaus Fuchs sketched the type of bomb that was dropped on Hiroshima, Japan.

by the deep growling roar of the explosion, his face relaxed into an expression of tremendous relief. The effects could well be called unprecedented, magnificent, beautiful, stupendous, and terrifying. The explosion came . . . pressing hard against the people and things, to be followed almost immediately by the strong, sustained, awesome roar which warned of doomsday and made us feel that we puny things were blasphemous to dare tamper with the forces reserved for the Almighty."

Just three weeks later, three American B-29 superfortresses took off from the tiny island of Tinian in the Pacific. Japanese radar picked them up off the coast, but just three planes seemed harmless. Nothing was done to intercept the flight.

One of the planes, the *Enola Gay*, sped ahead of the accompanying aircraft as they neared Hiroshima. Her crew members put on colored glass goggles, a "weaponeer" made a last-minute adjustment in the bomb bay. Then the aircraft commander, Colonel Paul Tibbetts, Jr., wheeled the *Enola Gay* over the city, and a single bomb was dropped. The plane turned and sped back towards Tinian. It was at least ten miles away when the atomic bomb went off, and a terrifying flash lit up the sky.

An old army tent was thrown over the bomb, and Bacher, Oppenheimer, and a few others huddled under it next to the awesome device while lightning crackled around the tall steel tower on which the bomb was to be mounted.

Luckily it did not strike. The bomb was successfully armed, hoisted to the top of the tower, and early on the morning of the sixteenth a countdown started. A War Department release later described the situation:

"Dr. Oppenheimer grew tenser as the seconds ticked off . . . and then when the announcer shouted 'now' and there came this tremendous burst of light followed immediately

Tibbetts later described what had happened: "There was a mushroom, of course, and under it the city seemed to just be a black, billowing layer of boiling tar."

Most of Hiroshima was simply gone, and a new force had imposed itself, for good or evil, on the world.

But if the atom had its terrifying aspects, it also had good ones. Medicine found dozens of uses for putting the atom to work. A whole industrial technology sprang up, based on the use of radioactive "tracers" which can be used to detect everything from the whereabouts of engine oil to the thickness of metal parts. Proposals were made that small "clean" bombs could be used to blast out harbors.

Perhaps even more important, nuclear reactors promise man a ready source of power when his natural resources—oil, coal, and wood —are exhausted.

The principle of a reactor is quite simple: the heat given off by uranium or plutonium, in which a controlled chain reaction is taking place, is absorbed by water, which turns to steam. And steam, as we know, can be turned into electricity with a turbine wheel and a dynamo.

Steam can be used to spin propellers, too. In 1955, the world's first atomic vessel, the submarine *Nautilus*, was launched. Early in 1961

The world's first atomic reactor was built by Italian physicist Enrico Fermi.

the *Savannah*, the first atomic merchant ship, will go to sea, powered by a heavy chunk of atomic fuel.

Just around the corner the awesome power of fusion waited to be unleashed. For when the nuclei of the lighter elements like hydrogen are jammed together or fused (rather than being split or fissioned, as in the atomic bomb), they become heavier than they were separately. The excess weight turns into enormous energy—much, much more than fission releases.

It takes millions of degrees of heat to get the nuclei together, though, so fusion ordinarily takes place only in a hydrogen bomb, which uses an A-bomb trigger to provide the heat necessary. Scientists are now at work inventing "magnetic bottles" (any

kind of ordinary container would be melted by the terrific heat) to hold the atoms together. When this controlled fusion becomes practical, man will have an inexhaustible supply of fuel at his finger tips, for plain sea water will provide the fuel for the fusion reactors of the future.

Was the splitting of the atom an invention? Most scientists think so. Enrico Fermi and his Italian colleagues shared $300,000 for work they did in 1934. In 1940, Charles Dunham and a group of Columbia University scientists patented their method for separating pure U-235 from the ordinary U-238. Their patent suit is still pending, but if it is granted, the cash award to the inventors could be in the neighborhood of one billion dollars.

The men who first suspected the existence of unknown particles in the atom might very well have agreed with today's scientists. "The greatest inventions," Benjamin Franklin once said, "are those inquiries which tend to increase the power of man over matter." Certainly by this definition the splitting of the atom is the greatest invention of all.

A ghostly blue glow (known as Cerenkov radiation) lights up the pool of water shielding the core of Tennessee's Oak Ridge Research Reactor. The reactor is used to test the effects of radiation on fuels and metals. It also produces radioisotopes used in industry, agriculture, and in medical and biological research.

PROBING THE UNIVERSE

For years scientists "looked" at the atom, and it seemed very small. It would take six million of them, they found, to make an atomic necklace two feet long, and even then most of that would be empty space. But when man began to look at the universe around him with improved telescopes, what he saw made him feel extremely small himself.

The earth, he found, is just a tiny bit of cosmic dust compared to the universe—a small planet circling a minor sun perched on the edge of a galaxy called the Milky Way. The Milky Way contains roughly thirty billion suns, or stars, and it is itself only one of about a hundred million galaxies in the known universe.

These astronomical figures might well have shocked even Galileo and Newton, for the early telescopes could focus on only a tiny fraction of these stars. Not until 1920, in fact, did man prove that many of the stars the early astronomers saw belonged not to the Milky Way, but to other galaxies trillions of miles away.

So vast are the distances involved that man has simplified the problem of writing down all the zeroes by expressing celestial distances in "light years." A "light year" is the distance which light, moving at 186,326 miles per second, travels in one year. Our closest neighboring galaxy,

Andromeda, is still more than 900,-000 light years away.

Europe's early astronomers concerned themselves mostly with our own solar system, the sun, its planets, and their moons. Their telescopes were too primitive to get a good look at anything else.

They used what are now called refracting telescopes or "refractors," in which light passes directly to the eye through a series of lenses mounted in a tube. One problem with these early refractors was that they produced colors around the edges which blurred the image.

In 1671 Isaac Newton built a new kind of telescope. In his reflecting telescope, or "reflector," the rays from a distant object are concentrated and reflected by a mirror. The resulting beam is then reflected off another mirror to an eyepiece on the tube's side.

In the eighteenth century, instrument-makers discovered how to make lenses which produced images devoid of color. For about one hundred years refractors became the most popular instrument. Then men learned how to make mirrors better by putting a thin layer of silver over glass, and reflectors returned to favor. Today most giant telescopes are reflectors since refractors' huge lenses may sag from their own weight, while reflectors' mirrors

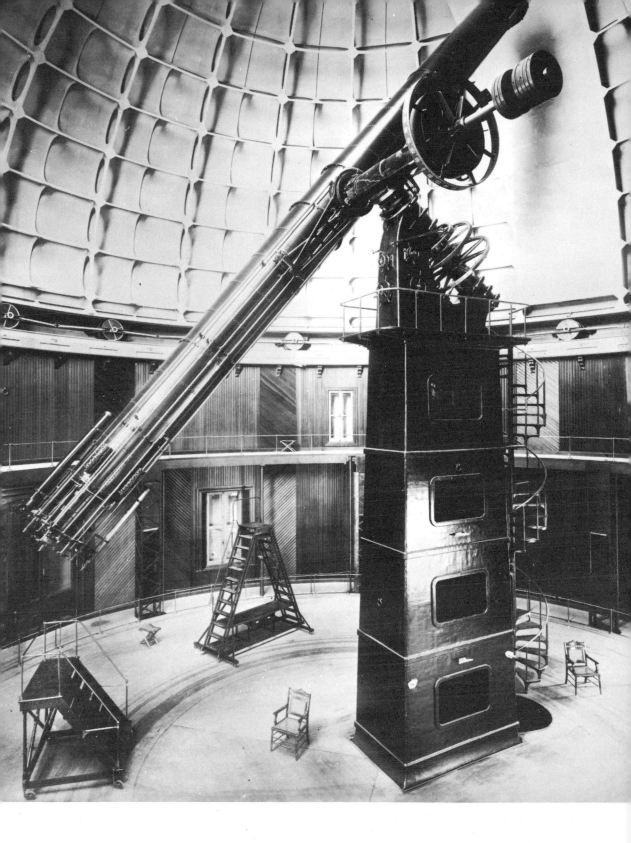

The great refracting telescope at the Lick Observatory on Mt. Hamilton, California, was finished in 1888. It was the most powerful telescope of its time.

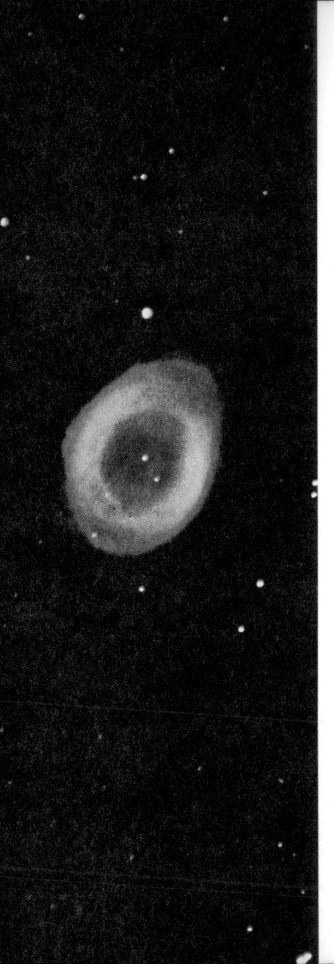

The pictures on these pages were taken by the 200-inch Hale telescope. The Ring Nebula—a fluorescent rainbow of gases in the constellation Lyra—is seen here.

can be braced from behind.

In Europe many observatories were built over the years, but in America progress was slow. In 1825 President John Quincy Adams complained that America had no "lighthouses of the skies."

Slowly, throughout the 1830's and 1840's, observatories began to appear in the United States. The country's earliest permanent observatory was set up at Williams College in 1838. A comet that flashed over New England in 1843 so intrigued Bostonians that they raised the money to give Harvard its first observatory. From then on American astronomy advanced by rapid strides.

Much of this advance was due to a portrait painter named Alvan Clark. In 1844, Clark became so intrigued watching one of his sons polish the reflector for a small telescope that he gave up painting for a career as a maker of mirrors and lenses. One of his refracting telescopes was used to detect the two moons of Mars in 1877.

When Clark died, his son, Alvan G. Clark, ran the telescope shop. During the 1880's, he started grinding the lenses for a 40-inch refractor for the University of California, but unfortunately, they canceled the order when a gift of money they had expected was not received.

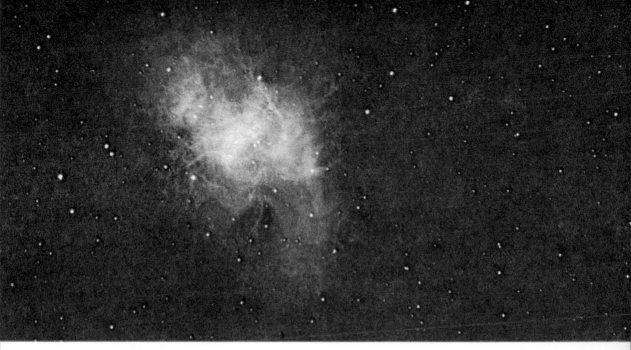

The explosion of the star which formed the Crab Nebula (above) was seen by Chinese astronomers in 1054 A.D. This photograph shows the vast cloud of gases which resulted. It is still expanding at the rate of 70 million miles per day.

At a scientific meeting, Clark turned to a young astronomer, George Ellery Hale, for help. Hale was a fine astronomer, and he had invented the spectroheliograph, which could be used to photograph accurately different parts of the sun's atmosphere.

Hale was as good as a fund raiser as he was as an astronomer and inventor. He persuaded Charles Yerkes, a Chicago streetcar magnate, who had acquired his fortune dishonestly, to give the money for the telescope. Yerkes was agreeable—he wanted to redeem himself with the people of Chicago—and thus, the University of Chicago acquired its famous Yerkes Observatory.

In 1903, Hale moved his family to Pasadena, California. Nearby was 6,000-foot high Mt. Wilson, a perfect spot, he thought, for a telescope. So, in 1906, he persuaded John D. Hooker, a Los Angeles businessman, to give the money for a 100-inch reflecting telescope.

The Hooker telescope gave the first accurate measurement of the diameter of a star, Betelgeuse, in the constellation Orion. Betelgeuse was found to be so large that if our sun were at its center, the earth would orbit wholly within its envelope of fiery gases.

The 100-inch scope also revealed to the astronomer Edwin Powell Hubble the true nature of spiral nebulae. These fuzzy, pinwheel-shaped objects had long been discussed by puzzled astronomers.

Hubble took photographs of the Andromeda Nebula showing individual stars embedded in it. Thus he proved nebulae were galaxies, or clouds of stars like the Milky Way, which contains all the stars we can see with our naked eyes.

Another leading American astronomer of the early 1900's, was Percival Lowell, of the famous Boston family. In the early 1890's, Lowell heard that the keen eyesight of the Italian astronomer, Giovanni Schiaparelli, had failed. Before this happened, Schiaparelli thought he saw a number of shadowy, fine lines crisscrossing the surface of the planet Mars. He called these lines, *canali*, "channels."

Lowell determined to take up the study of Mars where Schiaparelli left off. At his own expense, he built an observatory on a mesa in Arizona. Lowell argued that the *canali* were canals made by intelligent human beings; the Martians, he claimed, had dug the canals to bring water to the desert regions from the polar wastes of their planet.

Later observations made Lowell's theories extremely unlikely. His observatory, however, has made a number of important discoveries, and the existence of the planet Pluto, sighted by Clyde Tombaugh in 1930, had been predicted by Lowell many years before.

Another of America's great observatories was founded through the generosity of James Lick of California. Upon his death in 1876, Lick left $700,000 of his fortune to be used to build an instrument "superior and more powerful than any telescope yet made."

Alvan Clark's sons made the lenses for the then huge 36-inch refractor of the Lick Observatory on Mount Hamilton, and it has been studying the heavens ever since 1888. In 1960, a 120-inch reflecting telescope, perhaps the last of the big optical telescopes to be built in this country, was constructed nearby.

The Hooker 100-incher dwarfed the first Lick telescope, but George Hale still was not satisfied. In the 1920's, he felt the time had come to build the biggest telescope possible.

He found that a 200-inch reflector —that is, one with a mirror 16 feet 8 inches in diameter—could be both built and moved. That was all Hale needed to know. Again he raised the money, this time from the Rockefeller General Education Board and from the industrialist Andrew Carnegie. An enormous disc of pyrex glass to serve as the telescope's mirror was ordered from the Corning Glass Works in upstate New York.

Molding the huge chunk of glass was a difficult task, and after it was finished, the great lens was nearly shattered by an earthquake and washed away by floods. Finally, in 1936, it was shipped to California on a special railroad car. The job of grinding and polishing the mirror was halted by World War II, but it was finally finished and trucked up Mount Palomar in 1947.

The 200-inch telescope could look two *billion* light years into space, and it seemed for a while that this would be the limit to man's view of the heavens, for larger optical telescopes were impractical.

But in 1931 a Bell Telephone Company scientist had begun the research that would lead to a telescope that could "see" twenty times as far. Karl Jansky discovered in that year that a great deal of radio noise was coming in from space, some of it even from our own sun.

This was very interesting, for visible light—radiation that we can see with our eyes—is only a very small part of the total radiation that pours into the earth from space. We know now that the invisible radiations—which cause static on your radio—can be every bit as revealing to an astronomer as is the light coming

These "big dishes" at Owens Valley, California, are the 90-foot antennae for a radio telescope that can "listen" to stars billions of miles away.

Around 1800, Sir William Congreve began to develop military rockets for the English army. Soldiers are shown here testing Congreve's new weapon.

in from the stars that we can see.

The instruments developed over the years to pick up and record this radiation are called radiotelescopes. Basically, they consist of a huge antenna, usually saucer-shaped, and an amplifier to boost the weak signals detected by the antenna. The radiotelescope built at Sugar Grove, West Virginia, in 1960 has an antenna 600 feet across made from 20,000 tons of steel.

This instrument can look 38 billion light years, some 228 billion, billion miles, into space.

Before this information is discovered, however, man is liable to be launching himself into space at least as far as the moon in a device first invented by the Chinese—the rocket.

The Chinese improvised their "arrows of flaming fire" around the seventh century, A.D., not long after they invented the gunpowder to fuel them. Their rockets were not unlike the skyrockets used in fireworks demonstrations today.

Gunpowder reached the Western World about the middle of the thirteenth century, and before long, Europeans were toying with rockets.

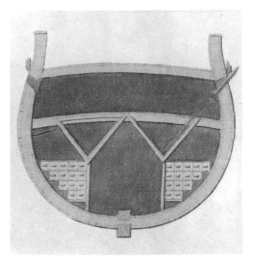

Rockets were soon widely used by the British navy. The cross section (above) of a British warship shows a rocket in the "scuttle" ready for firing. British rocket ships (below) are engaged in the kind of bombardment they hurled against Ft. McHenry in the War of 1812.

This illustration foretold—by more than ninety years—mankind's launching of animals into space. It appeared in Jules Verne's science fiction adventure From the Earth to the Moon *published in 1865.*

For 250 years, they were quite popular as incendiary weapons for setting fire to ships and towns. But during the sixteenth century, cannon were improved to the point where the erratic rockets seemed old-fashioned.

For a long time, they became toys in the hands of fireworks makers. Then, about 1800, an Englishman named William Congreve began inventing rockets.

His rockets were still crude, but with them, he managed to set fire to Boulogne and Copenhagen in England's war against Napoleon of France. Congreve's rockets were also used against the Americans in the War of 1812. His flaming missiles inspired Francis Scott Key to write, as the siege of Fort McHenry in Baltimore, of "the rockets' red glare, the bombs bursting in air."

All these rockets used solid fuel to propel them according to Newton's third law: "every action has an equal and opposite reaction." As the powder burned, it created gases which expanded and rushed out a nozzle at one end of the rocket. The rocket would then react by shooting off in the opposite direction.

The jet engine works on the same principle as the rocket, but a rocket carries the oxygen needed for combustion along with it, while a jet mixes the oxygen in the air with the fuel it carries. Thus, an airplane can fly only within the earth's atmosphere, while a rocket, or a rocket plane can roar along through the near vacuum of space.

Just as Congreve's rockets started making a name for themselves, cannon were improved again. Their barrels were rifled, as those of the Kentucky rifles had been, for accuracy. Once again rockets were abandoned as weapons.

Then, in the 1890's, a shy, self-educated Russian schoolteacher, Konstantine Eduoardovitch Tsiolkovsky, started thinking about space travel.

Tsiolkovsky realized that only one kind of engine would work in the vacuum of space—a "reaction" engine—and he set about designing one powered by liquid fuels, which were much more efficient than the solids. The Russian never actually tried to build one of his engines, but he wrote many important works on rocket engines and space travel.

While Tsiolkovsky was writing what then seemed like fantasy, an American boy named Robert Goddard was dreaming about flight.

Fifty years later, when the American Army questioned the German rocket scientist, Wernher von Braun,

and asked him how he made his V-2 missiles, he replied: "Ask your own Doctor Goddard."

Goddard's first successful missile was an anti-tank rocket that was shot from a tube four-and-a-half feet long. Today we call the modern version of his invention a bazooka. The inventor had bigger things on his mind, though, and he began to think about rockets that could actually escape from earth's gravity. In 1920

On March 16, 1926, Dr. Robert Goddard—with one hand resting on his launching apparatus—posed for this photograph. He was ready to set off the world's first liquid-fueled rocket. Moments later, the rocket rose forty feet into the air.

The large B-52 jet plane (left) has just launched the smaller X-15 rocket plane from beneath her wing. First released at an altitude of 38,000 feet, the rocket has since broken all speed and altitude records for manned flight. Tiros I (right) was boosted into orbit on April 1, 1960. The satellite has since taken and transmitted to earth thousands of photographs of the globe and its enveloping cloud cover.

the Smithsonian Institution published his paper, "A Method of Reaching Extreme Altitudes," and a *New York Times* story headlined: BELIEVES ROCKET CAN REACH MOON!

In a follow-up story, the *Times's* editorial writer, who apparently had never studied Newton, chided Goddard for perpetrating the "hoax" that rockets can travel in a vacuum.

Goddard was, of course, completely right. In fact, a rocket travels better in a vacuum than it does in the air, because its speed depends on how fast its exhaust gases are shot out. In a vacuum, with nothing to push against, they go faster than they do in air.

Goddard came in for more criticism when his first experiments on liquid-fueled engines went awry. But, in 1926, Goddard finally had a rocket that he thought would fly. It was about ten feet high, mostly tubing with a couple of skyrocket-like gadgets inside—the motor slung above the propellant tanks.

On a cold winter day in March, Goddard toted his apparatus to a farm near Auburn, Massachusetts, and set it up in the middle of a snow-covered pasture. He fueled it carefully with gasoline and liquid oxygen (a pipe led from each fuel tank to a combustion chamber, where the two would mix and burn). Goddard started a ten-second countdown, and one of his assistants, Henry Sachs, ignited the rocket with a blowtorch strapped onto the end of a long pole.

At the count "one . . . Go!" the rocket wavered, shot up for about forty feet, turned over on its side, then roared across the field, and crashed in a cabbage patch 185 feet away.

That short, erratic flight was the world's first for a liquid-fueled rocket, and before long, Goddard had bigger and better ones going up. He

had to move out to New Mexico—away from fire marshals and the police—to shoot off the really big ones. In 1935, one of Goddard's rockets soared up 7,500 feet.

By that time, rockets were becoming popular again. The American Rocket Society, founded in 1930, had some highly successful shoots from the beaches of Staten Island in New York. In Germany, a man named Hermann Oberth, submitted his doctoral thesis at Heidelberg on the subject of space travel, and a German Rocket Society was formed. As early as 1929, many of its members were put to work building rockets for military purposes. One of them was a man not yet twenty years old, who had worked for Oberth, Baron Wernher von Braun.

In 1942, after many failures and partial successes, one of their V (for vengeance) 2's soared 125 miles and landed on target. The success had been achieved in spite of Hitler's initial opposition to the project.

The V-2 rocket reached England in great numbers, but fortunately it was not in time to win the war for Germany. After the war, many of the Germans, von Braun among them, came to America to work on missiles and research rockets.

By 1955, American scientists had progressed to the point where they thought they could orbit an artificial earth satellite during the International Geophysical Year (IGY) that began in July of 1957.

But, as it turned out, the Russians brought man to the edge of the Space Age. On October 4, 1957, a 184-pound "sputnik" was put into orbit. Not long afterwards, the Russians launched one around the sun, and then one around the moon. Another Soviet probe smacked into the middle of the moon itself. In the same years, more than twenty American earth satellites went up, a small fourteen-pound package joined the Red satellite Mechta in orbit around the sun, and another man-made moon was in orbit around Venus.

The idea of satellites was not exactly new. Philosophers of the eighteenth century had suggested that rockets might be used to put them up into orbit.

Man has already learned a great deal from satellites—that the earth is faintly pear-shaped, that it is ringed with bands of intense radiation, that the temperature inside a satellite can be regulated easily to make it comfortable for man.

Americans have advanced from their primitive wind and water mills to atomic reactors and manned rockets in less than 400 years—not long when you think that life has existed on earth for millions of years.

Invention is no longer a matter of survival to Americans. We have the farm and factory machinery we need to feed and clothe ourselves, and American industry can turn out as many gadgets and luxuries as her citizens can afford to buy.

Pioneer V, launched on February 29, 1960, radioed back information on cosmic conditions until it had traveled 22,500,000 miles into space. Its radio transmitter was powered by means of the solar cells on its four paddles which converted the energy of sunlight into electricity.

What science and invention will do next we do not know. Perhaps the great age of science that began with Isaac Newton will come to an end before atomic-powered interplanetary rockets appear. The world has gone through dark ages before, and there may again come a time when man wishes to destroy the machines he has brought into being.

Perhaps the most important thing Americans have learned in their short history is that they cannot go on forever importing their scientists from Europe and mass-producing hardware based on a fund of knowledge accumulated in other parts of the world. The result is that American science has taken enormous strides in the twentieth century.

Learning the secrets of the space and atom worlds will not be easy. It will take, as Edison put it, more perspiration than inspiration. But at least we now know that perfection in science and invention is impossible, and that there is much left to invent and even more to discover. And the more we learn, the more we realize how little we really know. That is the healthiest possible sign for American science.

AMERICAN HERITAGE PUBLISHING CO., INC. · BOOK DIVISION: Richard M. Ketchum, *Editor*. JUNIOR LIBRARY: Ferdinand N. Monjo, *Editor*, John Ratti, *Assistant Editor*. Malabar Schleiter · Judy Sheftel · Julia B. Potts · Mary Leverty, *Editorial Assistants. Designed by Joseph Trautwein*.

ACKNOWLEDGMENTS   The editors are deeply grateful to Dr. Robert P. Multhauf, Head Curator of Science and Technology at the Smithsonian Institution, both for his assistance in the preparation of the text as well as for his guidance and advice on pictorial material and sources. In addition, they wish expressly to thank the following individuals and organizations for their generous assistance and for their cooperation in providing pictorial matter from their collections: Franklin Institute—Mr. Albert Hollingsworth; New York Historical Society—Mr. Arthur Carlson; Edison Laboratory National Monument—Mr. Norman Speiden; NASA—Mr. John Zimmerman; Newsweek Magazine—Mrs. Deborah Link; Mr. Philip Van Doren Stern of Brooklyn; and Mr. Robert Honeyman of New York City.

PICTURE CREDITS

The source of each picture used in this book is listed below, by page. When two or more pictures appear on one page, they are separated by semicolons. The following abbreviations are used:

IAS—Institute of Aeronautical Science, N.Y.C.
SI—Smithsonian Institution.
MMA—Metropolitan Museum of Art.
FI—Franklin Institute, Philadelphia.
LC—Library of Congress.
NYPL—New York Public Library.
APS—American Philosophical Society, Philadelphia.

ELNM—Edison Laboratory National Monument, Orange, N. J.
CIT—California Institute of Technology, Pasadena, California.
NASA—National Aeronautic and Space Administration, Washington, D. C.
IBM—International Business Machines, Inc.

Cover: "Awaiting the Reply" by Robert Dudley—SI, MMA. **Front end sheet:** Engine side taken from the Hand Pump Fire Engine of the Franklin Volunteer Fire Co. of Philadelphia—Insurance Co. of North America. **5** Wright glider, 1902—IAS. **6** From *Treasures of Art, Industry, and Manufacture*—MMA. **9** Harvard University. **10–11** NYPL. **12** Science Museum, London. **13** (top) Yale University; (bot.) MMA, Rogers Fund. **14–15** Walker Art Gallery, Liverpool, Eng. **16** With credit and copyright Life and Eliot Elisofon, 1956 Time Inc. **17** SI. **18–19** "Eleutherian Mills" by Bass Otis—Eleutherian Mills-Hagley Foundation, Wilmington, Del. **20** NYPL. **22–23** IBM. **25** Library Co. of Philadelphia. **26** (top) FI; (center left) FI; (center right) NYPL; (bot.) Harvard University. **27** NYPL. **28** FI. **29** Old Print Shop. **31** (top) U.S. Patent Office; (bot.) *Complete Works of Count Rumford*, 1870. **32** Kennedy Galleries. **34** (top left) APS; (right) Joseph Kindig Coll.; (bot. left) University of Pennsylvania Lib. **36** (top left) Harvard University; (top right) Fogg Art Museum, Harvard University; (bot. left) APS; (bot. right) APS. **38–39** Mabel Brady Garven Coll., Yale University. **40** (top left) SI; (top center and top right) gift of Mrs. F. Durand, MMA; (bot.) University of Michigan, Transportation Lib. **41** SI. **42–43** Hulton Picture Library, London. **44** (both) Stevens Institute. **45** (top) Cooper Union; (bot.) LC. **46–47** (top) NYPL; (bot.) New Jersey Historical Soc. **48** (top) SI; (bot.) gift of Mrs. F. Durand, MMA. **49** SI. **50** Mabel Brady Garven Coll., Yale University. **51** SI. **52** American Antiquarian Soc. **54–55** Chicago Historical Soc. **56** Colt Patent Fire Arms Mfg. Co. **57** (top) U.S. Steel Corp.; (bot.) Deere & Co., Moline, Ill. **58–59** "Forging the Shaft, A Welding Heat" by John F. Weir—gift of L. G. Bloomingdale, MMA. **60** (above) SI; (below) Science Museum, London. **61** LC. **63** Drake Memorial Museum, Titusville, Pa. **64–65** (both) Drake Memorial Museum. **66–67** Automotive Collection of Philip Van Doren Stern. **68** Henry Ford Museum, Dearborn, Mich. **70** (top) NYPL; (bot.) Peoria Public Library, Ill. **71** (top left) Hulton Picture Library; (top right) Henry Ford Museum; (bot.) Long Island Automotive Museum, Southampton, N.Y. **73** Courtesy of the Royal Aeronautical Society, London. **75** National Air Museum, Washington, D.C. **76** IAS. **77** LC. **78** LC. **79** Underwood & Underwood. **80–81** Museum of the City of New York. **82** Princeton University Lib. **84** (top) Bettmann Archives; (center) Princeton University Lib.; (bot.) SI. **86** SI. **87** LC. **88** National Academy of Design, N.Y.C. **89** (all) SI. **90** U.S. National Museum, Washington, D.C. **91** (both) LC. **92–93** SI-MMA. **94–95** (both) American Telephone & Telegraph Co. **96–97** (both) SI. **98** (top) SI; (bot.) ELNM. **99** ELNM. **100** LC. **101** (top) Culver Service; (bot.) Free Library of Philadelphia. **103** Chicago Historical Society. **104** (trolley) Frank Rowsome Jr.; (bot. left) Otis Elevator Co.; (bot. right) NYPL. **106** (top) Remington Rand Corp.; (bot.) LC. **107** New York Historical Soc. **108** ELNM. **109** ELNM. **110–111** NYPL. **112** Yale University. **113** General Electric Co. **114–115** Steelways Magazine. **116** IBM. **118–119** New York Historical Soc. **120** Science Museum, London. **121** Ernst Haas—Magnum. **122–123** Brookhaven National Laboratory, Upton, N.Y. **124–125** (both) Brown Bros. **125–127** Anscochrome by Erwin W. Muller. **128** CIT. **129** Culver Service. **131** Atomic Energy Commission. **132** London Daily Express. **133** Wide World. **134–135** Union Carbide Corp. **137** LC. **138** CIT. **139** CIT. **141** CIT. **142–143** (top, left) Robert Honeyman Coll.; (top: right, and bottom) National Maritime Museum, England. **144** NYPL. **145** Coll. of Mrs. Robert H. Goddard. **146** North American Aviation, Inc. **147** NASA. **149** NASA. **Back end sheet:** Andromeda Galaxy—CIT. **Back cover:** (top) Mabel Brady Garven Coll., Yale University; (center left) New York Historical Soc.; (center right) NYPL; (bot. left) Courtesy of the Royal Aeronautical Society; (bot. right) Bettmann Archives.

Bathe, Greville, and Bathe, Dorothy. *Oliver Evans; A Chronicle of Early American Engineering.* Philadelphia: The Historical Society of Pennsylvania, 1935.

Boyd, Thomas. *Poor John Fitch.* New York: G. P. Putnam's Sons, 1935.

Burlingame, Roger. *Machines That Built America.* New York: Harcourt, Brace & Co., 1953.

Chambre, René. *Histoire de L'Aviation.* Paris: Flammarion, 1949.

Clagett, Marshall. *Greek Science in Antiquity.* New York: Abelard-Schuman, Inc., 1955.

Clark, J. Stanley. *The Oil Century.* Norman, Oklahoma: University of Oklahoma Press, 1958.

Clarke, Arthur C. *Voice Across the Sea.* New York: Harper & Brothers, 1958.

Cohen, I. Bernard. *The Birth of a New Physics.* Garden City, N. Y.: Doubleday & Co., Inc., 1960.

Cohen, I. Bernard. *Some Early Tools of American Science.* Cambridge, Mass.: Harvard University Press, 1950.

Cooke, David C. *The Story of Aviation.* New York: Archer House, 1958.

Dampier, William. *A History of Science and its Relation with Philosophy.* Cambridge, England: The University Press, 1942.

Denison, Merrill. *The Power To Go.* Garden City, N. Y.: Doubleday & Co., Inc., 1956.

Dolson, Hildegarde. *The Great Oildorado.* New York: Random House, 1959.

Farber, Eduard. *The Evolution of Chemistry.* New York: Ronald Press Co., 1952.

Fermi, Laura. *Atoms In the Family.* Chicago, Ill.: University of Chicago Press, 1954.

Forbes, R. J. *Man the Maker.* New York: Abelard-Schuman, Inc., 1958.

Franklin, Benjamin. *Autobiographical Writings,* ed. Carl Van Doren. New York: Viking Press, 1952.

Fuller, Edmund. *Tinkers and Genius.* New York: Hastings House, 1955.

Gartmann, Heinz. *Rings Around the World.* New York: William Morrow & Co., 1959.

Giedion, Siegfried. *Mechanization Takes Command.* New York: Oxford University Press, 1948.

Glasstone, Samuel. *Sourcebook on Atomic Energy.* Princeton, New Jersey: D. Van Nostrand Co., Inc., 1958.

Hall, Arthur R. *The Scientific Revolution: 1500–1800.* London: Longmans, Green & Co., Inc., 1954.

Hindle, Brooke. *The Pursuit of Science in Revolutionary America.* Chapel Hill, North Carolina: University of North Carolina Press, 1956.

Holton, Gerald, and Roller, Duane. *Foundations of Modern Physical Science.* Reading, Mass.: Addison-Wesley Publishing Co., Inc., 1958.

Jaffe, Bernard. *Men of Science in America.* New York: Simon & Schuster, 1958.

Josephson, Matthew. *Edison.* New York: McGraw-Hill, 1959.

Josephson, Matthew. *The Robber Barons.* New York: Harcourt, Brace & Co., 1934.

Jungk, Robert. *Brighter Than a Thousand Suns.* New York: Harcourt, Brace & Co., 1958.

King, Henry Charles. *The History of the Telescope.* London: Griffin, 1955.

Klemm, Friedrich. *A History of Western Technology.* New York: Charles Scribner's Sons, 1959.

Lang, Daniel. *From Hiroshima to the Moon.* New York: Simon & Schuster, 1959.

Ley, Willy. *Rockets, Missiles, and Space Travel.* New York: Viking Press, 1957.

Maclaurin, W. Rupert. *Invention and Innovation in the Radio Industry.* New York: Macmillan Co., 1949.

Milbank, Jeremiah. *The First Century of Flight in America.* Princeton, N. J.: Princeton University Press, 1943.

Mirsky, Jeannette, and Nevins, Allan. *The World of Eli Whitney.* New York: Macmillan Co., 1952.

Nevins, Allan. *Ford, the Times, the Man, the Company.* New York: Charles Scribner's Sons, 1954.

Oliver, John W. *History of American Technology.* New York: The Ronald Press, 1956.

Pendray, Edward G. *Men, Mirrors, and Stars.* New York: Funk & Wagnalls Co., 1935.

Pledge, H. T. *Science Since 1500.* New York: Harper & Brothers, 1959.

Romer, Alfred. *The Restless Atom.* Garden City, N. Y.: Doubleday & Co., Inc., 1960.

Schamehorn, Howard. *Balloons to Jets.* Chicago: Henry Regnery Co., 1957.

Smith, David. *History of Mathematics,* Vol. I. New York: Dover Publications, 1951.

Smith, David. *History of Mathematics,* Vol. II. New York: Dover Publications, 1953.

Thompson, James A. *Count Rumford of Massachusetts.* New York: Farrar & Rinehart, Inc., 1935.

Turnbull, Archibald D. *John Stevens, an American Record.* New York: The Century Co., 1928.

Usher, Abbott P. *A History of Mechanical Inventions.* Boston: Beacon Press, 1959.

Van Doren, Carl. *Benjamin Franklin.* New York: The Viking Press, 1952.

Wheeler, Lynde P. *Josiah Willard Gibbs.* New Haven: Yale University Press, 1951.

Wolf, A. *A History of Science, Technology, and Philosophy in the 16th and 17th Centuries,* Vol. I. New York: Harper & Brothers, 1959.

Woodbury, David. *Beloved Scientist.* New York: McGraw-Hill, 1944.

FOR FURTHER READING

Young readers seeking further information on men of science and invention will find the following books to be both helpful and entertaining:

Ahnstrom, D. N. *Complete Book of Jets and Rockets.* Cleveland: World Publishing Co., 1957.

Caldwell, Cyril. *Henry Ford.* New York: Messner, 1948.

Charnley, Mitchell V. *Boys' Life of the Wright Brothers.* New York: Harper & Brothers, 1928.

Cousins, Margaret. *Ben Franklin of Old Philadelphia.* New York: Random House, 1952.

Garbedian, H. Gordon. *Thomas Alva Edison: Builder of Civilization.* New York: Messner, 1947.

Haber, Heinz. *Our Friend the Atom.* New York: Simon & Schuster, 1956.

Hart, Ivor B. *James Watt and the History of Steam Power.* New York: Abelard, 1949.

Hogben, Lancelot. *The Wonderful World of Energy.* Garden City, N. Y.: Garden City Books, 1957.

Lewellen, John. *The Boy Scientist.* New York: Simon & Schuster, 1955.

Lewellen, John, and Shapiro, Irwin. *The Story of Flight.* New York: Golden Press, 1959.

Stevenson, O. J. *Talking Wire. The Story of Alexander Graham Bell.* New York: Messner, 1947.

Throm, Edward. *The Boy Engineer.* New York: Golden Press, 1959.

Tunis, Edwin. *Wheels: A Pictorial History.* Cleveland: World Publishing Co., 1955.

Watson, Jane Werner. *The World of Science.* New York: Golden Press, 1958.

Wyler, Rose, and Ames, Gerald. *The Golden Book of Astronomy.* New York: Simon & Schuster, 1958.

INDEX

Bold face indicates pages on which illustrations appear.